Hello Korean

Volume 2

A Language Study Guide for K-pop & K-drama Fans

Soyoung Yoo
Lee Joon-gi

TUTTLE Publishing

Tokyo | Rutland, Vermont | Singapore

Contents

A Message from the Author

Thanks to the Hallyu Korean wave, more and more people today are learning Korean. In fact, when I ask students who come to my university to study Korean why they're learning the language, many of them tell me that it's because they like Korean stars like Lee Joon-gi or BTS.

This got me thinking, wouldn't it be great if someone made a book that would allow people to study Korean with a Hallyu star? And then Lee Joon-gi came along to help me turn this dream into a reality.

When *Hello Korean Volume 1* was published, the response was more enthusiastic than I had expected. I got to meet all sorts of people studying Korean because of the book—not only foreigners and exchange students in Korea, but people from around the world through various social media channels. I heard from people not just in Japan, China, and other Asian countries, but also residents of Europe, the Middle East, North America, and Africa, and we also received feedback on how to improve the book from people who had studied with it. One young student from Uganda showed an unusual degree of affection for the book, remarking, "When I go back to Uganda to become a Korean teacher, I really want to use this book in my classroom." I appreciate the passion shown by all of these people.

It is a delight to see the book starting to receive recognition not only from individual learners, but also from academic and educational institutions. I am grateful for all these amazing responses, and at the same time I feel an even greater responsibility as an author.

If *Hello Korean Volume 1* was an introduction to Korean that focused on providing complete beginners with a foundation for learning the language, this book, *Hello Korean Volume 2*, puts the focus on helping learners use more natural Korean expressions and sentence structures in their daily life. Learners are encouraged to spend time focusing on the "Conversation Practice" and "Let's Practice" sections and also to try applying what they learn in real situations. Do this, and you will find your Korean speaking ability improving much faster.

I am so happy to see my students in the classroom studying with this book—and with the actor I love. I wish you all the very best.

—Soyoung Yoo

A Message from Lee Joon-gi

After *Hello Korean Volume 1* was first published in Korea—before it became available all over the world—I had to do my military service, so there was a gap before we could start working on *Hello Korean Volume 2*. Fortunately, I made it through the service without any serious mishaps and was happy to be able to start work on the second volume. I felt that the students who had been studying with the first volume must have got really good at Korean while I was off doing my military service! I was touched to hear that so many people were studying Korean using *Hello Korean Volume 1*.

The recording work that I did for the first volume was fun and laid-back. It felt almost like I was wrapping up a present I wanted to surprise readers with. But with this book, I felt a little more pressure. No doubt part of this was the fact that the Korean learning material is more advanced than in the first volume, but it was also because I knew how passionately and diligently you were studying the language.

I want to express my gratitude to all of you overseas who are learning Korean through the *Hello Korean* series! In order to show how much I value your passion, I really worked hard on the recordings for this book, reading through the scripts whenever I had a spare moment in my busy schedule and kept repeating my lines over and over again. I almost felt like I had become a Korean teacher!

While it may be easy to start learning Korean as a foreign language, there's nothing easy about becoming good at Korean. If you ever feel stuck, please think of me as though I'm by your side, cheering you on! We've done our best to represent you in this book, with new characters from places all around the globe such as the Middle East, France, the US and Kenya.

I hope this book will make you even more interested in Korea and the Korean language. And as for me—I'm getting ready to bring you even better dramas and films. See you on the big screen!

—Lee Joon-gi

How to Use This Book

A lot of effort was made to ensure that explanations are easy enough for self-study students while focusing on basic vocabulary and expressions, challenging grammar points, as well as pronunciation rules.

- We abbreviated nouns to N, adjectives to A, and verbs to V in the text.
- Lee Joon-gi himself recorded all of his parts in the soundtrack.
- The answer key for the grammar exercises, conversation exercises, and listening exercises in each chapter is in the appendix .
- The rules of Korean pronunciation are covered comprehensively in *Hello Korean Volume 1*, pages 20–45. Every lesson in *Hello Korean Volume 2* has a Pronunciation Rules section, drawing your attention to various aspects of native-Korean pronunciation.
- Answers for the exercises and translations of audio scripts can be found at the back of the book.
- Online audio files for this book can be found at the link below. Each chapter of this book has its own audio file, labeled with the chapter number. All dialogues, vocabulary lists and listening practice exercises that have online audio files are marked with a logo of a student wearing headphones. The number underneath the logo indicates the point (in minutes and seconds) where that particular recording begins.

To Access the Online Recordings for This Book:

1. Check to be sure you have an internet connection.
2. Type the URL below into your web browser:

www.tuttlepublishing.com/hello-korean-v2

For support, you can email us at info@tuttlepublishing.com.

The Strengths of This Book

1. It's easy to study Korean no matter where you are

This book is a self-study Korean textbook designed for those who are learning on their own. The helpful explanations and wide range of exercises in the book make it simple to study the language wherever you may be. In addition, the book includes a variety of activities, making it possible for Korean teachers to use it in the classroom as well.

2. Studying Korean with this book makes use of all the senses, making it fun to learn

The *Hello Korean* series covers a number of learning approaches, including the voice of Hallyu star Lee Joon-gi, eye-catching illustrations, neatly arranged tables, exercises covering numerous expressions and grammar points, pair and groupwork activities and writing composition exercises, to help make studying Korean more fun.

3. The book is built upon the author's years of classroom experience and the perspectives of numerous Korean learners

The author uses her many year's of experience, as well as feedback from learners around the globe about *Hello Korean Volume 1*, to present grammar points and activities in a clear and easy-to-understand manner.

4. Actor Lee Joon-gi makes Korean study a new and more enjoyable experience

Who wouldn't enjoy studying while listening to the entertaining stories and soothing voice of actor Lee Joon-gi? There are many activities in the book that allow you to have conversations with Lee Joon-gi, which is fun and rewarding.

How This Book Is Organized

❶ Dialogue

Each chapter begins with a dialogue highlighting natural-sounding Korean expressions that can be used in everyday life. Use the online audio files to practice reading these dialogues aloud, as though you are having an actual conversation. Before you know it, Korean expressions will start coming to you effortlessly as you speak. Memorizing the entire dialogue is another great way to get better at Korean.

❷ Vocabulary and Expressions

While the lessons in *Hello Korean Volume 1* were built around the vocabulary taught in each chapter, the lessons in Book 2 include not only new vocabulary to be learned but also a variety of other words that are either related to the key vocabulary or that are worth learning in general. In particular, we have included a lot of vocabulary and expressions that are closely connected to everyday life.

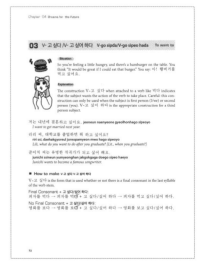

❸ Grammar

If you have mastered the grammar in *Hello Korean Volume 1*, this book will take your grammar skills to the next level, with detailed grammar explanations, example sentences and opportunities for practice, to help you move closer to native-like fluency.

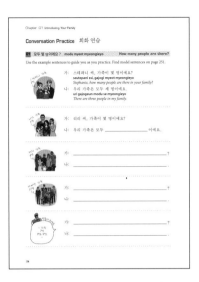

❹ Conversation Practice

You'll have many opportunities in this book to practice a variety of Korean expressions that are commonly encountered in everyday life. At the end of each chapter, there is a practice section, where you can make your own sentences, with plenty of examples and prompts to inspire you.

❺ Listening Practice

This book will build on the listening skills you developed in *Hello Korean Volume 1* to help you develop your fluency in understanding spoken Korean. While all listening exercises in this book have tapescripts, try listening first without looking at the text, to challenge yourself. You might be surprised to find how quickly your understanding of spoken Korean will improve!

❻ Talking with Lee Joon-gi

The audio recordings by Lee Joon-gi in every chapter are the springboard for a wide range of activities including conversation practice, writing letters, composing descriptive pieces and carrying out interview. Lee Joon-gi's charming voice is sure to inspire and motivate you!

❼ Let's Practice

We have included a "Let's Practice" section at the end of every chapter so that you can place yourself in a variety of situations as you practice common, everyday expressions. These sections work particularly well if you have a Korean-speaking partner to practice with.

❽ Lee Joon-gi's Guide to Korea

In *Hello Korean Volume 1*, Lee Joon-gi introduced readers to some of the hot spots of Seoul. In this book, he takes you to some of the most fascinating destinations in Korea. Curious about what makes these places so charming? Join Mr. Lee to find out more!

Characters in the Book

최지영   이준기   리리   비비엔   퍼디   스테파니

1 Jiyoung Choi
최지영 choejiyeong

Korea

university student

2 Lee Joon-gi
이준기 ijungi

Korea

movie actor

3 Lili
리리 riri

China

reporter

4 Vivien
비비엔 bibien

Germany

exchange student

5 Ferdy
퍼디 peodi

Philippines

university student

6 Stephanie
스테파니 seutepani

Australia

office worker

7 **Benson**

벤슨 benseun

Kenya

soccer player

8 **Hazuki**

하즈키 hajeuki

Japan

university student

9 **Jonathan**

요나단 yonadan

America

musician

10 **Henri**

앙리 angni

France

painter

11 **Amani**

아마니 amani

Saudi Arabia

announcer

12 **Junichi**

준이치 junichi

Japan

airline employee

Summary of Lesson Content

	Title	Key Language
1과	가족 소개 *Introducing Your Family*	*This Is My Father and Mother*
2과	첫인상 *First Impressions*	*She's a Pretty, Kind Person*
3과	계획 세우기 *Future Plans*	*What Are You Going to Do During Your Vacation?*
4과	미래를 위한 꿈 *Dreams for the Future*	*I Want to Be a Teacher*
5과	길 묻기 *Asking for Directions*	*Where is Kyobo Bookstore?*
6과	택시에 타서 *Taking a Taxi*	*Please Take Me to Insadong*
7과	전화 걸기 *Making a Phone Call*	*Is This Ferdy's House?*
8과	진찰받기 *Seeing a Doctor*	*I Have a Headache and a Cough*
9과	거절하기 *Declining a Request*	*I'm Sorry, but I Can't Go*
10과	옷차림 말하기 *Describing What Someone Is Wearing*	*She's the Person in the Yellow Dress*
11과	달라진 것 이야기하기 *Talking about Changes*	*The Weather Has Gotten Colder*
12과	할 수 있는 것 말하기 *Expressing What You Can Do*	*Can You Eat Spicy Food?*

Grammar	Vocabulary and Expressions	Pronunciation Rules
N 명/ N 사람/ N 분 N(이)랑 N N께서, N께서는	*Family, jobs*	*Nasalization of obstruents*
N을/를 좋아하다/싫어하다 무슨 N, 어떤 N A-(으)ㄴ/는 N	*Personality, appearance, preferences*	*Silent* ㅎ
A/V-(으)면 V-(으)ㄹ 거예요	*Leisure activities, feelings*	*Tensification*
N(이)군요! A-군요!V-는군요! N이/가 되다 V-고 싶다/V-고 싶어 하다	*Jobs*	*Liaison*
V-다가 N(으)로, N쯤	*Streets, locations, directions*	*Tensification*
V-아/어 주세요 A/V-(으)ㄹ테니까 N 안에	*Transportation, traffic*	*Silent* ㅎ
N의 N, N(이)지요? A/V-지요? N인데, V-는데, A-(으)ㄴ데	*Leisure activities*	*Nasalization of obstruents*
V-아/어도 되다 V-(으)면 안 되다	*Medical professionals, hospitals, diseases, medication, symptoms, parts of the body*	*Aspiration*
V-(으)러 가다/오다 A/V-아/어서	*Sports, excuses and reasons, places*	*Palatalization*
V-고 있다 V-는 N	*Colors, clothes, accessories, verbs for clothing*	*How to pronounce the vowel* 의
A-아/어지다 N1보다 N2 A/V-(으)ㄹ 때, A/V-았/었을 때	*Places, physical appearance*	*Tensification*
V-(으)ㄹ 수 있다/없다 못/안 V-아/어요	*Food, flavors, activities*	*Tensification*

THE LESSONS

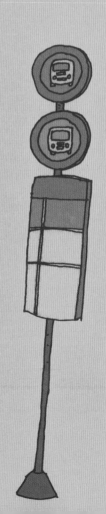

Introducing Your Family
가족 소개

우리 어머니랑
아버지예요
**This Is My
Father and
Mother**

Learning Objective

Situation
Introducing your
family
Vocabulary
Family
Jobs
Grammar
Counting units
And, with
Subject particle
(honorific)

ONLINE
AUDIO
00:45

최지영 choejiyeong	요나단 씨, 가족이 몇 명이세요? **yonadan ssi, gajogi myeot myeongiseyo** *Jonathan, how many people are in your family?*
요나단 yonadan	우리 가족은 모두 여섯 명이에요. **uri gajogeun modu yeoseot myeongieyo** *There are six people in my family altogether.*
	할아버지와 할머니가 계시고, 어머니와 아버지가 계세요. **harabeojiwa halmeoniga gyesigo, eomeoniwa abeojiga gyeseyo** *There is my grandfather and grandmother, and my father and mother.*
	그리고 동생이 하나 있어요. **geurigo dongsaengi hana isseoyo** *I also have one younger sibling.*
최지영 choejiyeong	아버지는 무엇을 하세요? **abeojineun mueoseul haseyo** *What does your father do?*
요나단 yonadan	우리 아버지는 의사예요. 병원에서 일하세요. **uri abeojineun uisayeyo. byeongwoneseo ilhaseyo** *My father is a doctor. He works at a hospital.*
최지영 choejiyeong	동생은 뭐 해요? **dongsaengeun mwo haeyo** *What does your sibling do?*
요나단 yonadan	제 동생은 대학생이에요. 마인츠 대학교에 다녀요. **je dongsaengeun daehaksaengieyo. maincheu daehakgyoe danyeoyo** *My sibling is a university student. (She/he) goes to Mainz University.*

Vocabulary and Expressions 어휘와 표현

ONLINE AUDIO
02:30

01 가족 gajok   **Family**

할머니 [할머니]
halmeoni
grandmother

할아버지 [하라버지]
harabeoji
grandfather

외할머니 [외할머니]
oehalmeoni
maternal grandmother

외할아버지 [외하라버지]
oeharabeoji
maternal grandfather

고모 [고모]
gomo
aunt
(father's sister)

삼촌 [삼촌]
samchon
uncle

아버지 [아버지]
abeoji
father

어머니 [어머니]
eomeoni
mother

이모 [이모]
imo
aunt
(mother's sister)

오빠 [오빠]
oppa
older brother
(of a female)

언니 [언니]
eonni
older sister
(of a female)

나 [나]
na
me

여동생 [여동생]
yeodongsaeng
younger sister

남동생 [남동생]
namdongsaeng
younger brother

형 [형]
hyeong
older brother
(of a male)

누나 [누나]
nuna
older sister
(of a male)

나 [나]
na
me

형제 [형제]
hyeongje
brothers

자매 [자매]
jamae
sisters

남매 [남매]
nammae
brother and sister

딸 [딸]
ttal
daughter

아들 [아들]
adeul
son

ONLINE AUDIO
03:35

02 직업 1 jigeop 1   Jobs 1

유치원생 〔유치원생〕 **yuchiwonsaeng** *kindergarten student*
*초등학생 〔초등학쌩〕 **chodeunghaksaeng** *elementary school student*
*중학생 〔중학쌩〕 **junghaksaeng** *middle school student*
*고등학생 〔고등학쌩〕 **godeunghaksaeng** *high school student*
*대학생 〔대:학쌩〕 **daehaksaeng** *university student*
경찰관 〔경찰관〕 **gyeongchalgwan** *police officer*
소방관 〔소방관〕 **sobanggwan** *firefighter*
*우체부 〔우체부〕 **uchebu** *postman*
스튜어디스 〔스튜어디쓰〕 **seutyueodiseu** *flight attendant*

* In 학생, /ㅎ/ is actually pronounced as an intermediate sound somewhere between /ㅎ/ and /ㅇ/.

03 동사 dongsa   Verbs

하다 〔하다〕 **hada** *to do*
있다 〔읻따〕 **itda** *to be (somewhere), to have*
계시다 〔계시다/게시다〕 **gyesida** *to be (somewhere, honorific)*
일하다 〔이라다〕 **ilhada** *to work*
다니다 〔다니다〕 **danida** *to go somewhere regularly, to attend*

04 기타 gita   Miscellaneous

명 〔명〕 **myeong** *person (counting word)*
몇 명 〔면명〕 **myeot myeong** *How many people?*
모두 〔모두〕 **modu** *altogether, all*
마인츠 대학교 **maincheu daehakgyo** 〔마인츠대학꾜〕 *Mainz University*

발음규칙 Pronunciation Rules

Nasalization of obstruents 장애음의 비음화
Obstruent sounds are sounds made by obstructing airflow such as /f/ or /k/. When the final consonant of a syllable is ㄱ, ㄷ, or ㅂ and the initial sound of the next syllable is ㄴ or ㅁ, it is pronounced as ㅇ, ㄴ or ㅁ.

$$몇 \, 명 \Rightarrow 〔면명〕$$

ㄷ(ㅅ,ㅆ,ㅈ,ㅊ,ㅌ,ㅎ) + ㅁ,ㄴ ⇒ ㄴ+ㅁ,ㄴ

다섯 명 다선명 **daseot myeong** *five people*   여섯 명 여선명 **yeoseot myeong** *six people*
일곱 명 일곰명 **ilgop myeong** *seven people*   아홉 명 아홈명 **ahop myeong** *nine people*

Grammar 문법

01 N 명, N 사람, N 분
N myeong, N saram, N bun
Counting units

Situation

You have a lot of friends, and you want to count them. You can say, 한 명, 두 명, 세 명 . . . or 한 사람, 두 사람, 세 사람 . . .

Explanation

We use the constructions N 명, N 사람 and N 분 to count people. N 명 and N 사람 can be used interchangeably for friends and other people we are close to. N 분, on the other hand, is a respectful expression that is used in a formal setting.

■ 몇 명? myeot myeong **How many people?**

1	2	3	4	5	6
한 명	두 명	세 명	네 명	다섯 명	여섯 명
han myeong	du myeong	se myeong	ne myeong	daseot myeong	yeoseot myeong

7	8	9	10	11	12
일곱 명	여덟 명	아홉 명	열 명	열한 명	열두 명
ilgop myeong	yeodeol myeong	ahop myeong	yeol myeong	yeolhan myeong	yeoldu myeong

■ 몇 사람? myeot saram **How many people?**

1	2	3	4	5	6
한 사람	두 사람	세 사람	네 사람	다섯 사람	여섯 사람
han saram	du saram	se saram	ne saram	daseot saram	yeoseot saram

7	8	9	10	11	12
일곱 사람	여덟 사람	아홉 사람	열 사람	열한 사람	열두 사람
ilgop saram	yeodeol saram	ahop saram	yeol saram	yeolhan saram	yeoldu saram

■ 몇 분? myeot bun How many people (honorific)?

1 한 분 **han bun**	2 두 분 **du bun**	3 세 분 **se bun**	4 네 분 **ne bun**	5 다섯 분 **daseot bun**	6 여섯 분 **yeoseot bun**
7 일곱 분 **ilgop bun**	8 여덟 분 **yeodeol bun**	9 아홉 분 **ahop bun**	10 열 분 **yeol bun**	11 열한 분 **yeolhan bun**	12 열두 분 **yeoldu bun**

02 N(이)랑 N   N (i)rang   And/with

Situation

Vivien and Ferdy are here, together. To express this you say: 비비엔이랑 퍼디가 있어요.

Explanation

N(이)랑 N is a grammatical structure that joins two different nouns together in a group. In this sense, it means the same thing as N 그리고 N. Thus, 사과랑 바나나 means 사과, 그리고 바나나. Compared to N하고 N, which you learned in the previous volume, this structure sounds more casual and is often used with close friends.

책상 위에 커피랑 바나나가 있어요.
chaeksang wie keopirang bananaga isseoyo
There's a coffee and some bananas on the desk.

저기에 비비엔이랑 퍼디가 와요.
jeogie bibienirang peodiga wayo
Vivien and Ferdy are there.

비비엔이랑 퍼디

주말에 명동이랑 인사동에 가요.
jumare myeongdongirang Insadonge gayo
(I) go to Myeongdong and Insadong at the weekend.

■ **How to make** N(이) 랑 N

When there is a final consonant in the last syllable of the noun, use N이랑. When there is not, use N랑.

Final Consonant + 이랑: 비빔밥/고기 → 비빔밥이랑 불고기

No Final Consonant + 랑: 사과/바나나 → 사과랑 바나나

03 N 께서 /N 께서는 N kkeseo/N kkeseoneun Subject particle (honorific)

Situation

You want to know what Grandfather is doing. You say: 할아버지께서 뭐 하세요? Grandfather is reading the newspaper. You say: 할아버지께서는 신문을 읽으세요. Mother is cleaning. You say: 어머니께서는 청소하세요.

Explanation

N께서 and N께서는 are both honorific expressions, and typically the N slot is filled with someone older than the speaker, such as a grandfather, grandmother, father, mother or teacher. N께서 is the respectful equivalent of the particle N이/가, while N께서는 is the respectful equivalent of the particle N은/는.

아버지께서 뭐 하세요? **abeojikkeseo mwo haseyo**
What is your father doing?

선생님께서 영화를 보세요. **seonsaengnimkkeseo yeonghwareul boseyo**
The teacher is watching a movie.

어머니께서는 요리하세요. **eomeonikkeseoneun yorihaseyo**
My mother is cooking.

■ How to make N께서/N께서는

Regardless of whether or not the last syllable of the noun has a final consonant, you can use N께서 and N께서는.

Final Consonant + 께서/께서는: 선생님 → 선생님께서, 선생님께서는

No Final Consonant + 께서/께서는: 할아버지 → 할아버지께서, 할아버지께서는

활용 연습 Usage Practice

Fill in the blanks. Find the answers on page 251.

Base Form	N(이)랑
바나나/사과	바나나랑 사과
빵/우유	빵이랑 우유
학교/도서관	
선생님/학생	

Base Form	N께서	N께서는
외할아버지	외할아버지께서	외할아버지께서는
외할머니		
삼촌		
고모		

Conversation Practice 회화 연습

01 모두 몇 명이에요 ?   modu myeot myeongieyo   **How many people are there?**

Use the example sentences to guide you as you practice. Find model sentences on page 251.

가: 스테파니 씨, 가족이 몇 명이에요?
seutepani ssi, gajogi myeot myeongieyo
Stephanie, how many people are there in your family?

나: 우리 가족은 모두 세 명이에요.
uri gajogeun modu se myeongieyo
There are three people in my family.

가: 리리 씨, 가족이 몇 명이에요?

나: 우리 가족은 모두 _____ 이에요.

가: _____ ?

나: _____ .

가: _____ ?

나: _____ .

가: _____ ?

나: _____ .

02 모두 몇 분이세요 ? **modu myeot buniseyo**   **How many are you?**

Use the example sentences to guide you as you practice. Find model sentences on page 251.

가: 어서 오세요. 모두 몇 분이세요?
eoseo oseyo. modu myeot buniseyo
Hello. How many are you?

나: 모두 세 명이에요.
modu se myeongieyo
We are three.

가: 어서 오세요. 모두 몇 분이세요?

나: 모두 _____ 이에요.

가: _____ ?

나: _____ .

가: _____ ?

나: _____ .

만들어 보세요.

손님
4명/10명
8명
...

가: _____ ?

나: _____ .

| 03 | 우리 아버지랑 어머니예요.
uri abeojirang eomeoniyeyo | **They are my father and my mother.** |

Use the example sentences to guide you as you practice. Find model sentences on page 251.

가: 스테파니 씨, 이 사람들은 누구예요?
seutepani ssi, i saramdeureun nuguyeyo
Stephanie, who are these people?

나: 우리 아버지랑 어머니예요.
uri abeojirang eomeoniyeyo
They are my father and my mother.

기: 스테파니 씨, 이것은 뭐예요?
seutepani ssi, igeoseun mwoyeyo
Stephanie, what is this?

나: 지갑이랑 휴대폰이에요.
jigabirang hyudaeponieyo
It's my wallet and a mobile phone.

가: _____ , _____ ?

나: _____ .

가: _____ , _____ ?

나: _____ .

가: _____ , _____ ?

나: _____ .

04 할아버지께서는 무엇을 하세요 ?
harabeojikkeseoneun mueoseul haseyo
What does your grandfather do?

Use the example sentences to guide you as you practice. Find model sentences on page 251.

가: 할아버지께서는 무엇을 하세요?
harabeojikkeseoneun mueoseul haseyo
What does your grandfather do?

나: 할아버지는 우체부예요. 우체국에서 일하세요.
harabeojineun uchebuyeyo. uchegugeseo ilhaseyo
He is a postman. He works at the post office.

가: 형은 뭐 해요? **hyeongeun mwo haeyo**
What does your older brother do?

나: 형은 회사원이에요. 삼성에서 일해요.
hyeongeun hoesawonieyo. samseongeseo ilhaeyo
He is an office worker. He works at Samsung.

가: _____?

나: _____.

가: _____?

나: _____.

가: _____?

나: _____.

27

Listening Practice 듣기 연습

ONLINE AUDIO
05:39

Listen to the online audio file and match each member of Stephanie's family to one of the occupations in the pictures below by drawing a line to connect the dots. You can find the audio script on page 239.

문제 다음 그림에서 스테파니 씨 가족들의 직업을 찾아 연결하세요.

아버지
.

어머니
.

스테파니
.

남동생
.

.
요리사

.
우체부

.
의사

.
경찰관

.
대학생

.
중학생

Talking with Lee Joon-gi 이준기와 이야기하기

ONLINE AUDIO
07:48

Try having a conversation with Lee Joon-gi as you listen to the audio. You can find a translation of this conversation on page 245.

이준기   안녕하세요? 이것은 우리 가족사진이에요.

우리 가족은 모두 다섯 명이에요.

할아버지가 계시고, 아버지와 어머니가 계세요.

그리고 여동생이 하나 있어요.

우리 할아버지는 우체부예요.

우리 아버지는 의사예요. 병원에서 일하세요.

우리 어머니는 요리사예요. 레스토랑에서 일하세요.

여동생은 고등학생이에요. 한국고등학교에 다녀요.

그리고 저는 영화배우예요.

하즈키   안녕하세요? 이것은 우리 가족사진이에요.

우리 가족은 모두 세 명이에요.

아버지, 어머니가 계시고 그리고 저예요.

우리 아버지는 우체부예요. 우체국에서 일하세요.

우리 어머니는 선생님이에요. 학교에서 일하세요.

그리고 저는 대학생이에요. 한국대학교에 다녀요.

연습해 보기 Let's Practice

Paste a picture of your family in the box below and write some sentences to introduce them.

The picture of your family goes here.

이것은 우리 가족사진이에요.

_____

_____

_____

_____

_____

_____

_____

Lee Joon-gi's Guide to Korea

Jeonju Hanok Village

Hundreds of Hanoks Evoke the Old Days

What's a *hanok*, you ask? That's the term for a traditional Korean house. To see seven hundred such buildings, head to the hanok village located in Pungnap-dong in Jeonju. Spend some time contemplating the rows of houses with their old-fashioned roofs and savor a sense of tranquility. That's the biggest appeal of Korea's traditional houses.

But don't just stand outside the village. Inside, the Traditional Alcohol Museum and the Craft Exhibit Hall are well worth a visit, and you'll also find lots of antique sellers.

Drop into an old teahouse for a relaxing cup of tea, while you listen to the distant sound of music blending with birdsong and the sound of a burbling stream.

If you've seen the movie *A Promise*, you aren't likely to simply pass by beautiful Jeongdong Cathedral, also located in Jeonju. However, the thing that really sets this region apart is its famous bibimbap: rice mixed with red pepper paste and a savory blend of fresh greens.

Old-fashioned tiled roofs dominate this view of the hanok village.

Jeondong Cathedral is the backdrop for the movie A Promise.

함께 떠나요!

First Impressions
첫인상

Learning Objective

Situation
First impressions
Vocabulary
Personality
Appearance
Preferences
Grammar
To like/dislike
What kind of . . . ?
Modifiers

ONLINE
AUDIO
00:10

리리 riri	이준기 씨, 여자 친구가 있어요? **ijungi ssi, yeoja chinguga isseoyo** *Joon-gi, do you have a girlfriend?*	
이준기 ijungi	아니요, 없어요. **aniyo, eopseoyo** *No, I don't.*	
리리 riri	이준기 씨는 어떤 사람을 좋아하세요? **ijungi ssineun eotteon sarameul joahaseyo** *What kind of person do you like?*	
이준기 ijungi	저는 재미있는 사람을 좋아해요. **jeoneun jaemiinneun sarameul joahaeyo** *I like someone who's fun.*	
리리 riri	아! 그래요? 그럼, 제 친구를 소개해 드릴까요? **a! geuraeyo? geureom, je chingureul sogaehae deurilkkayo** *Oh, really? In that case, would you like me to introduce you to my friend?*	
이준기 ijungi	네, 좋아요. 그 사람은 어떤 사람이에요? **ne, joayo. geu sarameun eotteon saramieyo** *Yeah, sure. What kind of person is she?*	
리리 riri	얼굴이 예쁘고 친절한 사람이에요. **eolguri yeppeugo chinjeolhan saramieyo** *She is a kind person with a pretty face.*	
이준기 ijungi	네, 좋아요. 그럼, 언제 만날까요? **ne, joayo. geureom, eonje mannalkkayo** *Alright. So when shall we meet?*	
리리 riri	내일 오후 2시에 학교 앞 카페에서 만납시다. **naeil ohu 2sie hakgyo ap kapeeseo mannapsida** *Let's meet in the café in front of the school at 2 pm tomorrow.*	

Vocabulary and Expressions 어휘와 표현

ONLINE AUDIO
01:53

01 성격 seonggyeok   Personality

친절하다 〔친절하다〕 **chinjeolhada** *to be kind*
불친절하다 〔불친절히다〕 **bulchinjeolhada** *to be unkind*
착하다 〔차카다〕 **chakada** *to be nice*
못되다 〔몯ː뙤다〕 **motdoeda** *to be mean, to be bad*
말이 많다 〔마리만타〕 **mari manta** *to be talkative*
말이 없다 〔마리업따〕 **mari eopda** *to not say much*
시끄럽다 〔시끄럽따〕 **sikkeureopda** *to be loud, noisy*
조용하다 〔조용하다〕 **joyonghada** *to be quiet*
상냥하다 〔상냥하다〕 **sangnyanghada** *to be kind, gentle*
무뚝뚝하다 〔무뚝뚜카다〕 **muttukttukada** *to be curt*
재미있다 〔재미읻따〕 **jaemiitda** *to be fun*
재미없다 〔재미업따〕 **jaemieopda** *to not be fun*
머리가 좋다 〔머리가조타〕 **meoriga jota** *to be smart*
머리가 나쁘다 〔머리가나쁘다〕 **meoriga nappeuda** *to be stupid*
똑똑하다 〔똑또카다〕 **ttokttokada** *to be smart*

02 외모 oemo   Appearance

예쁘다 〔예쁘다〕 **yeppeuda** *to be pretty*
키가 크다〔키가크다〕 **kiga keuda** *to be tall*
뚱뚱하다〔뚱뚱하다〕 **ttungttunghada** *to be fat*
잘생기다〔잘생기다〕 **jalsaenggida** *to be handsome*
못생기다〔몯ː쌩기다〕 **motsaenggida** *to be ugly*
멋있다〔머딛따/머싣따〕 **meositda** *to be stylish*
얼굴이 둥글다〔얼구리둥글다〕 **eolguri dunggeulda** *to have a round face*

귀엽다〔귀엽따〕 **gwiyeopda** *to be cute*
키가 작다〔키가작따〕 **kiga jakda** *to be short*
날씬하다〔날씬하다〕 **nalssinhada** *to be skinny*

03 계절 gyejeol   Seasons

봄 〔봄〕 **bom** *spring*
가을 〔가을〕 **gaeul** *fall*

여름 〔여름〕 **yeoreum** *summer*
겨울 〔겨울〕 **gyeoul** *winter*

04 과일 gwail   Fruit

멜론〔멜론〕 **mellon** *melon*
포도〔포도〕 **podo** *grape*
귤〔귤〕 **gyul** *tangerine*

파인애플〔파이내플〕 **painaepeul** *pineapple*
복숭아〔복쑹아〕 **boksunga** *peach*
감〔감〕 **gam** *persimmon*

05 음식 eumsik   Food

된장찌개 〔된장찌개〕 **doenjangjjigae** *doenjang jjigae (fermented soybean stew)*

감자탕 〔감자탕〕 **gamjatang** *gamjatang (pork bone and potato stew)*

*떡 〔떡〕 **tteok** *rice cake*   치킨 〔치킨〕 **chikin** *fried chicken*

스파게티 〔스파게티〕 **seupageti** *spaghetti*   피자 〔피자〕 **pija** *pizza*

탕수육 〔탕수육〕 **tangsuyuk** *sweet-and-sour*   돈가스 〔동까스〕 **dongaseu** *pork cutlet*
　　pork

*Rice cake: This rice-based dish is an essential part of a baby's first birthday (돌), a parent's 60th birthday (회갑), the anniversary of a parent's death (기일), and any other important anniversary. In recent years, it is commonly eaten in place of a meal or as a snack, and it is also used to make "rice cake cake" (떡케이크) for someone's birthday.

06 기타 gita   Miscellaneous

어떤 사람 〔어떤사람〕 **eotteon saram** *what kind of person*

여자 (남자) 친구 〔여자칭구/남자칭구〕 **yeoja (namja) chingu** *girlfriend (boyfriend)*

소개하다 〔소개하다〕 **sogaehada** *to introduce*

소개해 드릴까요? 〔소개해드릴까요〕 **sogaehae deurilkkayo** *Would you like me to introduce . . . ?*

아! 그래요? 〔아그래요〕 **a! geuraeyo** *Oh, really?*

카페 〔카페〕 **kape** *café*

발음규칙 Pronunciation Rules

'ㅎ' 탈락 Silent ㅎ
When final consonant ㅎ is followed by a syllable beginning with ㅇ, the ㅎ is silent.

$$좋아요 \Rightarrow 〔조아요〕$$
$$ㅎ + ㅇ \Rightarrow \emptyset + ㅇ$$

좋아하세요 조:아하세요 **joahaseyo** *(She/he) likes.*
좋은 조 : 은 **joeun** *good.*
많아요 마 : 나요 **manayo** *(There are) many.*
많은 마 : 는 **maneun** *many*

Grammar 문법

01 N 을 / 를 좋아하다 / 싫어하다
N eul/reul joahada/sireohada

To like/dislike

Situation

You like the snow, and you like skiing. You like the winter! What you say: 저는 겨울을 좋아해요! You don't like the heat, and you don't like the rain. You don't like the summer! What you say: 저는 여름을 싫어해요!

Explanation

The constructions N을/를 좋아하다 and N을/를 싫어하다 are used to express likes and dislikes regarding food, exercise, fruit, seasons, or anything else. The corresponding construction in English is "to like N" and "to not like N."

저는 커피를 좋아해요. **jeoneun keopireul joahaeyo**
I like coffee.

저는 여름을 좋아해요. **jeoneun yeoreumeul joahaeyo**
I like summer.

저는 운동을 싫어해요. **jeoneun undongeul sileohaeyo**
I dislike exercise.

■ **How to make** N을/를 좋아하다, N을/를 싫어하다

Use N을 좋아하다/싫어하다 with nouns that have a final consonant and N를 좋아하다/싫어하다 with nouns that don't have a final consonant.

Final Consonant + 을 좋아하다/싫어하다: 겨울 → 겨울을 좋아해요/싫어해요.

No Final Consonant + 를 좋아하다/싫어하다: 바나나 → 바나나를 좋아해요/싫어해요.

02 무슨 N/ 어떤 N   museun N/eotteon N   What kind of . . . ?

Situation

You have a fruit, but you're not sure what it's called. You ask, 무슨 과일이에요? You know that the fruit is an apple, but you're not sure how it tastes: good or bad, sweet or sour. Here, you ask, 어떤 과일이에요?

Explanation

You can see that 무슨 is used to ask about the category or name of an object, while 어떤 is used to ask about the character or characteristics of a person or object. So what kind of nouns can fill the N slot in the grammatical constructions 무슨 N and 어떤 N? Basically, any nouns that represent a general category, such as "fruit" (representing apples, bananas, strawberries, and pineapples) or "coffee" (representing cappuccino, espresso, and café latte).

이것은 무슨 과일이에요? 바나나예요.
igeoseun museun gwairieyo? bananayeyo
What kind of fruit is this? It's a banana.

이것은 무슨 운동이에요? 수영이에요.
igeoseun museun undongieyo? suyeongieyo
What kind of sport is this? It's swimming.

슈퍼맨은 어떤 영화예요? 재미있는 영화예요.
syupeomaeneun eotteon yeonghwayeyo?
jaemiinneun yeonghwayeyo
What kind of movie is Superman? It is a fun movie.

■ How to make 무슨 N/어떤 N

Whether or not the noun has a final consonant, it is written as 무슨 N or 어떤 N.

Final Consonant: 무슨 과일(사과, 바나나 . . .) 어떤 과일(맛있는, 신 . . .)

No Final Consonant: 무슨 영화(왕의 남자, 괴물 . . .) 어떤 영화(슬픈, 재미있는 . . .)

03 A-(으)ㄴ/는 N   A-(eu)n/neun N   **Modifiers**

Situation

You're drinking a cappuccino and it's delicious. You say: 카푸치노는 맛있는 커피예요. You have a friend named Lili. She's pretty. You say: 리리 씨는 예쁜 사람이에요. These sentences are both present tense, telling us that the cappuccino is delicious right now, and Lili is pretty right now.

Explanation

A-(으)ㄴ/는N tells us what N is like by providing information about its current appearance or condition. In English, an adjective like "pretty" can be put in front of a noun like "person" without changing its form, as in "pretty person." Korean is a little more complicated, though, and the ending depends on whether the adjective root has a final consonant or not. Let's take a look at how this works in Korean.

저는 밝은 방을 좋아해요. **jeoneun balgeun bangeul joahaeyo**
I like a bright room.

저는 키가 큰 사람을 좋아해요. **jeoneun kiga keun sarameul joahaeyo**
I like tall people.

저는 달고 맛있는 복숭아를 좋아해요. **jeoneun dalgo masinneun boksungareul joahaeyo**
I like a sweet and tasty peach.

■ How to make A-(으)ㄴ/는 N

Adjectives with a final consonant take the form A-은 N, while adjectives without a final consonant take the form A-ㄴ N.

Final Consonant + 은 N: 많다/사람 → 많다 + 은 사람 → 많은 사람

No Final Consonant + ㄴ N: 예쁘다/사람 → 예쁘다 + ㄴ 사람 → 예쁜 사람

Final Consonant: ㄹ → ㄹ +ㄴ N: 달다/사과 → 달다 + ㄴ 사과 → 단 사과

Final Consonant: ㅂ → ㅂ 우+ㄴ N: 덥다/날씨 → 덥다 + 운(우 + ㄴ) 날씨 → 더운 날씨

~있다/없다 + 는 N: 맛있다/사과 → 맛있다 + 는 사과 → 맛있는 사과

활용 연습 Usage Practice

Fill in the blanks. Find the answers on page 251.

Base Form	A-(으)ㄴ/는 N	Base Form	A-(으)ㄴ/는 N
시다/레몬	신 레몬	밝다/방	
차갑다/녹차		예쁘다/여자	
달다/초콜릿		많다/사람	
힘들다/운동		친절하다/선생님	
재미있다/영화		귀엽다/동생	귀여운 동생
착하다/여자 친구		무뚝뚝하다/남자 친구	
작다/가방		춥다/날씨	
시끄럽다/장소		맑다/눈	

Conversation Practice 회화 연습

01 무슨 운동을 좋아하세요? **museun undongeul joahaseyo.** **What sports do you like?**

Use the example sentences to guide you as you practice. Find model sentences on page 251.

스키

가: 리리 씨, 무슨 운동을 좋아하세요?
riri ssi, museun undongeul joahaseyo
Lili, what sports do you like?

나: 저는 스키를 좋아해요.
jeoneun seukireul joahaeyo
I like skiing.

배구

가: 리리 씨, 무슨 _____ 을/를 좋아하세요?

나: 저는 _____ 을/를 좋아해요.

파인애플

가: _____ , _____ ?

나: _____ .

포도

가: _____ , _____ ?

나: _____ .

김밥

가: _____ , _____ ?

나: _____ .

돈가스

가: _____, _____?

나: _____.

만들어 보세요.

무슨 운동
태권도/배구
무슨 과일
사과/딸기
...

가: _____?

나: _____.

예

무슨 운동

골프
스키
농구
야구
배구
수영
태권도
축구
테니스

무슨 음식

된장찌개
비빔밥
김밥
돈가스
치킨
피자
떡

무슨 과일

파인애플
메론
바나나
포도
사과
배
딸기

| **02** | 슈퍼맨은 재미있는 영화예요.
 syupeomaeneun jaemiinneun yeonghwayeyo | **Superman is a fun movie.** |

Use the example sentences to guide you as you practice. Find model sentences on page 251.

슈퍼맨, 영화
 재미있다

가: 슈퍼맨은 어떤 영화예요?
syupeomaeneun eotteon yeonghwayeyo
What kind of movie is Superman?

나: 슈퍼맨은 재미있는 영화예요.
syupeomaeneun jaemiinneun yeonghwayeyo
It is a fun movie.

사과, 과일
 닮다

가: _____ 은/는 어떤 _____ 이에요?

나: _____ 과일이에요.

수영, 운동
 힘들다

가: _____?

나: _____.

떡볶이, 음식
 맵다

가: _____?

나: _____.

만들어 보세요.
어떤 n
불고기/음식
비싸다
왕의 남자/영화
슬프다
...

가: _____?

나: _____.

03 아마니 씨는 어떤 사람이에요?
amani ssineun eotteon saramieyo

What kind of person is Amani?

Use the example sentences to guide you as you practice. Find model sentences on page 252.

친절하다
똑똑하다

가: 아마니 씨는 어떤 사람이에요?
amani ssineun eotteon saramieyo
What kind of person is Amani?

나: 친절하고 똑똑한 사람이에요.
chinjeolhago ttokttokan saramieyo
She's kind and smart.

머리가
좋다
재미있다

가: 비비엔 씨는 _____?

나: _____ 사람이에요.

키가
작다
귀엽다

가: 스테파니 씨는 _____?

나: _____ .

똑똑하다
키가
크다

가: 리리 씨는 _____?

나: _____ .

만들어 보세요.
어떤 사람
상냥하다
매력있다
조용하다
얼굴이 둥글다
...

가: _____?

나: _____ .

Listening Practice 듣기 연습

ONLINE AUDIO
04:59

Listen to the online audio descriptions of Junichi and Lili, and draw them in the boxes below. You can find the audio script on page 239.

문제 준이치와 리리의 모습을 그려 보세요.

준이치	리리

Talking with Lee Joon-gi　이준기와 이야기하기

ONLINE AUDIO
07:59

Try having a conversation with Lee Joon-gi as you listen to the audio. You can find a translation of this conversation on page 245.

이준기	비비엔 씨, 한국 친구가 있어요?
비비엔	아니요, 없어요.
이준기	비비엔 씨는 어떤 사람을 좋아하세요?
비비엔	저는 키가 크고 친절한 사람을 좋아해요.
이준기	아! 그래요? 그럼, 제 친구를 소개해 드릴까요?
비비엔	네, 좋아요. 그 사람은 어떤 사람이에요?
이준기	제 친구는 조용하고 똑똑하고 친절한 사람이에요.
비비엔	네, 좋아요. 저는 똑똑한 사람을 좋아해요.
	그럼, 언제 만날까요?
이준기	그럼, 이번 주말에 명동에서 만납시다.
비비엔	네, 좋아요.

연습해 보기 Let's Practice

Look at the pictures below, and try asking and answering the suggested questions.

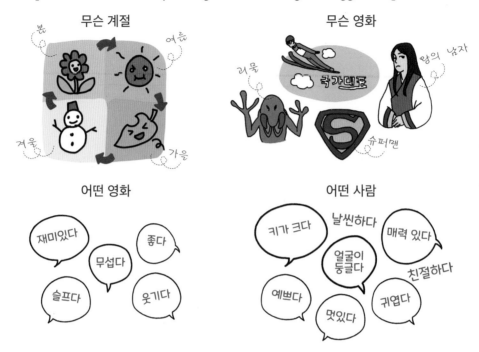

무슨 계절 / 봄 / 여름 / 겨울 / 가을

무슨 영화 / 괴물 / 국가대표 / 왕의 남자 / 슈퍼맨

어떤 영화 / 재미있다 / 무섭다 / 좋다 / 슬프다 / 웃기다

어떤 사람 / 키가 크다 / 날씬하다 / 매력 있다 / 얼굴이 둥글다 / 친절하다 / 예쁘다 / 멋있다 / 귀엽다

Fill in the chart with your ideas and create a conversation as the example shown below.

질문 question	친구 friend	
	1) 리리 Lili	2)
무슨 계절 *what season*	봄 *spring*	
무슨 영화 *what movie*	왕의 남자 *The King and the Clown*	
어떤 영화 *what kind of movie*	재미있다 *funny*	
친구 / 어떤 사람 *friend/ what kind of person*	착하다 *nice*	

가　리리 씨, 무슨 계절을 좋아하세요?

나　저는 봄을 좋아해요.

가　무슨 영화를 좋아하세요?

나　<왕의 남자>를 좋아해요.

가　<왕의 남자>는 어떤 영화예요?

나　재미있는 영화예요.

가　친구는 어떤 사람이에요?

나　착한 사람이에요.

Heyri Art Valley
The Most Beautiful Village on Earth

Drive through the open countryside and into Paju City in Gyeonggi Province to find Heyri Art Valley, a haven for Korea's artists. Koreans take pride in the fact that such a community exists for people involved in creating art and culture, just as the English are proud of cultural icons such as Shakespeare, the Beatles and Harry Potter. The name Heyri, it is said, comes from a folk story called *The Voice of Heyri*, which has been passed down for generations in the Paju region.

"The most beautiful village in the world" is something that artists only dream of. What is the deeper meaning of this dream? Is it the ambition to bring heaven to earth, or the drive to create great art? As they reflect on this question, visitors to this village can explore the charming buildings and works of art dotted here and there or take in one of the performances or art exhibits that are held nearly every day. A simple walk down the main street on a sunny afternoon is a true pleasure. We hope that the dreams and desires of the contemporary artists who live here will endure for a long, long time.

Heyri Art Valley is both retreat and inspiration for Korean artists.

Art exhibits that are held nearly every day.

Future Plans
계획 세우기

방학을 하면
뭐 할 거예요 ?
**What Are You
Going to Do
During Your
Vacation?**

Learning Objective

Situation
Future plans
Vocabulary
Leisure activities
Feelings
Grammar
If/when
Will/be going to

ONLINE
AUDIO
00:10

아마니 amani	앙리 씨, 방학을 하면 뭐 할 거예요?
	angni ssi, banghageul hamyeon mwo hal geoyeyo
	Henri, what are you going to do during school vacation?
앙리 angni	저는 방학을 하면 프랑스에 갈 거예요.
	jeoneun banghageul hamyeon peurangseue gal geoyeyo
	During the vacation, I'm going to go to France.
	아마니 씨는 방학을 하면 뭐 할 거예요?
	amani ssineun banghageul hamyeon mwo hal geoyeyo
	What are you going to do during vacation?
아마니 amani	저는 방학을 하면 아무것도 안 할 거예요.
	jeoneun banghageul hamyeon amugeotdo an hal geoyeyo
	During the vacation, I'm not going to do anything.
앙리 angni	어! 아마니 씨는 여행 안 갈 거예요?
	eo! amani ssineun yeohaeng an gal geoyeyo
	Huh? You're not going to go traveling?
아마니 amani	네, 그냥 집에서 푹 쉴 거예요.
	ne, geunyang jibeseo puk swil geoyeyo
	Yeah, I'm just going to get some rest at home.
	앙리 씨, 프랑스에서 예쁜 선물 사 오세요.
	angni ssi, peurangseueseo yeppeun seonmul sa oseyo
	Henri, bring me back a pretty present from France.
앙리 angni	네, 아마니 씨도 잘 지내세요. 다음 학기에 만나요.
	ne, amani ssido jal jinaeseyo. daeum hakgie mannayo
	OK. Take care of yourself. See you next semester.

Vocabulary and Expressions 어휘와 표현

ONLINE AUDIO
02:04

01 여가 yeoga   Leisure activities

방학을 하다 〔방하글하다〕 **banghageul hada** *to be on vacation from school*

사진을 찍다 〔사지늘찍따〕 **sajineul jjikda** *to take a picture*

쉬다 〔쉬다〕 **swida** *to rest*

늦잠을 자다 〔늗짜믈자다〕 **neutjameul jada** *to sleep in*

등산을 하다 〔등사늘하다〕 **deungsaneul hada** *to go hiking*

야구장에 가다 〔야구장에가다〕 **yagujange gada** *to go to a baseball game*

콘서트에 가다 〔콘서트에가다〕 **konseoteue gada** *to go to a concert*

*가야금을 배우다 〔가야그믈배우다〕 **gayageumeul baeuda** *to learn how to play the gayageum*

휴지를 줍다 〔휴지를줍따〕 **hyujireul jupda** *to pick up trash (lit., to pick up tissue)*

김치를 담그다 〔김치를담그다〕 **gimchireul damgeuda** *to make kimchi*

설거지를 하다 〔설거지를하다〕 **seolgeojireul hada** *to do the dishes*

침대에 눕다 〔침대에눕따〕 **chimdaee nupda** *to lie in bed*

* The gayageum is a traditional Korean musical instrument with either 12 or 25 strings.

02 동사 dongsa   Verbs

돌아오다 〔도라오다〕 **doraoda** *to come back*   취직하다 〔취지카다〕 **chwijikada** *to get a job*

만나다 〔만나다〕 **mannada** *to meet*   배우다 〔배우다〕 **baeuda** *to learn*

끝나다 〔끈나다〕 **kkeunnada** *to come to an end*

일등을 하다 〔일뜽을하다〕 **ildeungeul hada** *to come in first place*

03 형용사 hyeongyongsa   Adjectives

바쁘다 〔바쁘다〕 **bappeuda** *to be busy*

돈이 많다 〔도니만타〕 **doni manta** *to have a lot of money*

멀다 〔멀다〕 **meolda** *to be far*   가깝다 〔가깝따〕 **gakkapda** *to be close*

춥다 〔춥따〕 **chupda** *to be cold*   덥다 〔덥따〕 **deopda** *to be hot*

기분이 좋다 / 나쁘다 〔기부니조타 / 기부니나쁘다〕 **gibuni jota/nappeuda**
  to be in a good mood/to be in a bad mood

부럽다 〔부럽따〕 **bureopda** *to be envious, to be jealous*

무섭다 〔무섭따〕 **museopda** *to be scary*

시간이 있다 / 없다 〔시가니읻따 / 시가니업따〕 **sigani itda/eopda** *to have time/to have no time*

04 기타 gita **Miscellaneous**

방학 〔방학〕 **banghak** *school vacation*

아무것도 〔아무걷또〕 **amugeotdo** *nothing*

아무도 〔아무도〕 **amudo** *no one, nobody*

한 번도 〔함번도〕 **han beondo** *not once*

그냥 〔그냥〕 **geunyang** *just, as something is*

푹 〔푹〕 **puk** *a lot, well (often used with* **swida** 쉬다*)*

못 〔몯〕 **mot** *cannot*

선물 〔섬물〕 **seonmul** *present, gift*

아주 〔아주〕 **aju** *very*

소문 〔소문〕 **somun** *rumor*

부모님 〔부모님〕 **bumonim** *one's parents*

눈사람 〔눈:싸람〕 **nunsaram** *snowman*

눈싸움 〔눈:싸움〕 **nunssaum** *snowball fight*

드림 〔드림〕 **deurim** *"from" in a letter*

하지만 〔하지만〕 **hajiman** *but, however*

그래서 〔그래서〕 **geuraeseo** *so, for that reason*

발음규칙 Pronunciation Rules

경음화 Tensification '‿'
Tensification means making a sound tense. When the initial sound of a syllable following a verb or adjective ending in (으)ㄹ is ㄱ, ㄷ, ㅂ, ㅅ, or ㅈ, it is pronounced as ㄲ, ㄸ, ㅃ, ㅆ, and ㅉ.

$$할 거예요 \Rightarrow 〔할꺼예요〕$$
$$(으)ㄹ + ㄱ \Rightarrow (으)ㄹ + ㄲ$$

볼게 볼께 **bolge** *I will see (it).*
먹을 거예요 먹글꺼예요 **meogeul geoyeyo** *I will eat (it).*
볼수록 볼쑤록 **bolsurok** *the more I see (it)*
볼 줄 알다 볼쭐알다 **bol jul alda** *to know how to see (it)*

Grammar 문법

01 A/V-(으)면 A/V-(eu)myeon

If/when

Situation

You're on vacation next week and you're planning a trip. You say: 다음 주에 방학을 하면 여행을 가요. You're meeting a friend and planning to watch a movie. You say: 친구를 만나면 영화를 봐요.

* Note that while the basic meaning of A/V-(으)면 is "if," depending on the context, "when" is often a more appropriate translation.

Explanation

As in the sentences above, the A/V-(으)면 construction is used with expressions related to the future, such as "tomorrow," "this weekend" or "next year." The basic meaning of this construction is "Suppose _____ happens. In that case _____." This is not used with actions that have already been done or that are being done right now.

졸업을 하면 뭐 해요?
joreobeul hamyeon mwo haeyo
What are you going to do after you graduate?
[Lit. What do you do when you graduate?]

방학을 하면 여행을 가요.
banghageul hamyeon yeohaengeul gayo
I am going to travel during vacation. [Lit. I go to travel when my vacation begins.]

친구를 만나면 영화를 봐요.
chingureul mannamyeon yeonghwareul bwayo
I watch a movie when I meet my friend.

■ How to make A/V-(으)면

A/V-으면 is used when there is a final consonant in the last syllable of the verb or adjective stem. When there is no such consonant or when the final consonant is ㄹ, then A/V-면 is used with the verb or adjective.

Final Consonant + 으면: 먹다 → 먹다 + 으면 → 먹으면

No Final Consonant + 면: 만나다 → 만나다 + 면 → 만나면

Final Consonant + ㄹ + 면: 만들다 → 만들다 + 면 → 만들면

No Final Consonant + ㄷ → ㄹ + 으면: 듣다 → 듣다 + ㄹ으면 → 들으면

No Final Consonant + ㅂ → 우 + 면: 줍다 → 줍다 + 우면 → 주우면

활용 연습 I Usage Practice 1

Fill in the blanks. Find the answers on page 252.

Base Form	A/V-(으)면	Base Form	A/V-(으)면
방학을 하다	방학을 하면	바쁘다	바쁘면
시험이 끝나다		돈이 많다	
친구를 만나다		시간이 있다	
케이크를 만들다		날씨가 덥다	
소문을 듣다		기분이 좋다	
기분이 나쁘다		졸리다	
일이 끝나다		학교에 가다	
일등을 하다		무섭다	
침대에 눕다		집이 멀다	

02 V-(으)ㄹ 거예요 V-(eu)r geoyeyo   **Will/be going to**

Situation

You're planning to go swimming next weekend. You say: 저는 이번 주말에 수영을 할 거예요. You're on vacation next week and you're planning to go backpacking. You say: 다음 주에 방학을 하면 배낭여행을 할 거예요.

Explanation

The construction V-(으)ㄹ 거예요 allows us to express what we are planning to do in the future (this weekend, next month, next year). It isn't used about things that we have already done or are doing right now.

한국에 가면 뭐 할 거예요?
  hanguge gamyeon mwo hal geoyeyo
  What are you going to do when you go to Korea?

한국에 가면 태권도를 배울 거예요.
  hanguge gamyeon taegwondoreul baeul geoyeyo
  I am going to learn taekwondo when I go to Korea.

졸업을 하면 취직을 할 거예요.
  joreobeul hamyeon chwijigeul hal geoyeyo
  I am going to get a job after I graduate. [Lit. I am going to get a job when I graduate.]

시험이 끝나면 쉴 거예요. **siheomi kkeunnamyeon swil geoyeyo**
  I will rest when I finish my exams.

■ How to make V-(으)ㄹ 거예요

V-을 거예요 should be used when there is a final consonant in the last syllable of the verb stem. V-ㄹ 거예요 should be used when there is not.

Final Consonant + 을 거예요: 먹다 → 먹다 + 을 거예요 → 먹을 거예요.

No Final Consonant + ㄹ 거예요: 보다 → 보다 + ㄹ 거예요 → 볼 거예요.

Final Consonant + ㄹ → ㄹ + ㄹ 거예요: 만들다 → 만들다 + ㄹ 거예요 → 만들 거예요.

Final Consonant + ㄷ → ㄹ + 을 거예요: 듣다 → 듣다 + ㄹ을 거예요 → 들을 거예요.

Final Consonant + ㅂ → 우 + ㄹ 거예요: 줍다 → 줍다 + 울(우+ㄹ) 거예요 → 주울 거예요.

활용 연습 2 Usage Practice 2

Fill in the blanks. Find the answers on page 252.

Base Form	V-(으)ㄹ 거예요	Base Form	V-(으)ㄹ 거예요
여행을 하다	여행을 할 거예요.	수영을 하다	수영을 할 거예요.
사진을 찍다		음악을 듣다	
그림을 그리다		김치를 담그다	
쉬다		휴지를 줍다	
영화를 보다		가야금을 배우다	
비빔밥을 먹다		설거지를 하다	
책을 읽다		산책을 하다	
친구를 만나다		책상을 정리하다	
이메일을 보내다		잠을 자다	

Conversation Practice 회화 연습

01 방학을 하면 뭐 해요?
banghageul hamyeon mwo haeyo

What are you going to do during your vacation?

Use the example sentences to guide you as you practice. Find model sentences on page 252.

방학을 하다
제주도에 가다

가: 비비엔 씨, 방학을 하면 뭐 해요?
bibien ssi, banghageul hamyeon mwo haeyo
Vivien, what are you going to do during your vacation?
[Lit. Vivien, what do you do when your vacation begins?]

나: 저는 방학을 하면 제주도에 가요.
jeoneun banghageul hamyeon jejudoe gayo
I am going to Jeju Island during my vacation.
[Lit. I go to Jeju Island when my vacation begins.]

시간이 있다
여행을 하다

가: _____ 씨, _____ 뭐 해요?

나: _____ 여행을 해요.

한국말을 잘하다
한국어 선생님이 되다

가: _____ , _____ ?

나: _____ .

수업이 끝나다
콘서트에 가다

가: _____ , _____ ?

나: _____ .

숙제를 다하다
음악을 듣다

가: _____ , _____ ?

나: _____ .

바다에 가다
수영하다

가: _____ , _____ ?

나: _____ .

만들어 보세요.

가: _____ ?

나: _____ .

예

방학을 하다
고향에 가다

아침에 일어나다
요가를 하다

넓이섬에 가다
번지점프를 하다

시간이 있다
산책하다

＊〈준기 손잡고〉에 가다
가야금 공연을 보다

* Holding Hands with Joon-gi (준기 손잡고) is a yearly concert featuring fans of Lee Joon-gi. In this concert, fans perform music from Joon-gi's films and dramas that they have arranged for the traditional Korean instrument called the gayageum.

02 내일 민속촌에 갈 거예요.
naeil minsokchone gal geoyeyo

I am going to the folk village tomorrow.

Use the example sentences to guide you as you practice. Find model sentences on page 252.

내일
민속촌에 가다

가: 리리 씨, 내일 뭐 할 거예요?
riri ssi, naeil mwo hal geoyeyo
Lili, what are you going to do tomorrow?

나: 저는 내일 민속촌에 갈 거예요.
jeoneun naeil minsokchone gal geoyeyo
I am going to the folk village tomorrow.

내일
친구를 만나다

가: _____ 씨, _____?

나: 저는 _____ .

내일
번지점프를
하다

가: _____, _____ ?

나: _____ .

내일
야구장에 가다

가: _____, _____ ?

나: _____ .

주말
슈퍼에 가다

가: _____, _____ ?

나: _____ .

주말
김치를 담그다

가: _____ , _____ ?

나: _____ .

만들어 보세요.

가: _____ ?

나: _____ .

예 내일

TV를 보다

이준기를 만나다

동대문에 가다

예 주말

피아노를 치다

백화점

백화점에 가다

Listening Practice 듣기 연습

ONLINE AUDIO
05:08

Read the two questions below and then listen to the online audio file to find the answers, choosing from the illustrations. You can find the audio script on page 239.

문제 1 리리 씨는 이번 방학에 무엇을 할 거예요? 그림을 보고 고르세요.

문제 2 퍼디 씨는 이번 방학에 무엇을 할 거예요? 그림을 보고 고르세요.

Talking with Lee Joon-gi 이준기와 이야기하기

ONLINE AUDIO
07:57

Listen to Lee Joon-gi (on this page) and Viven (overleaf). Try having a conversation with Lee Joon-gi as you listen to the audio. Find translations of these two conversations on page 245.

이준기	여러분 안녕하세요? 이준기예요.
	저는 지금 시드니에서 영화 촬영을 하고 있어요.
	촬영이 끝나면 동물원에 가서 코알라를 만날 거예요.
	그리고 내일은 스테파니 씨를 만날 거예요.
	스테파니 씨가 수업이 끝나면 촬영장으로 올 거예요.
	우리는 같이 바다에 갈 거예요.
	바다에서 수영도 하고 맛있는 저녁도 먹을 거예요.
	여러분 즐거운 방학 보내세요.

비비엔   여러분 안녕하세요? 비비엔이에요.

저는 지금 파리에서 그림을 공부하고 있어요.

오늘 수업이 끝나면 친구들과 같이 에펠 탑에 갈 거예요.

우리는 에펠 탑에서 커피를 마시고 사진을 찍을 거예요.

저는 파리에서 그림 공부를 마치면 한국에 갈 거예요.

한국에서 디자이너가 될 거예요.

여러분, 한국에서 만나요.

연습해 보기 1 Let's Practice 1

Fill in the chart with your ideas and create a conversation between Jiyoung and friends as the example shown below.

질문 \ 친구	1) 스테파니
수업이 끝나다	친구를 만나다
친구를 만나다	영화를 보다

최지영 스테파니 씨, 수업이 끝나면 뭐 할 거예요?
스테파니 수업이 끝나면 친구를 만날 거예요.
최지영 친구를 만나면 뭐 할 거예요?
스테파니 친구를 만나면 영화를 볼 거예요.

질문 \ 친구	2)

질문 \ 친구	3)

연습해 보기 2 Let's Practice 2

Read Hazuki's letter below and use it as a model for writing your own.

사랑하는 부모님께. 안녕하세요? 일본은 요즘 날씨가 어때요?

여기 한국은 요즈음 춥고 눈이 많이 와요.

그래서 수업이 끝나면 친구들과 같이 눈사람도 만들고 눈싸움도 해요.

저녁에 집에 돌아오면 한국 TV를 봐요.

한국어는 아직 어렵지만 재미있어요.

이번 주말에 이준기 씨와 함께 제주도에 갈 거예요.

제주도에는 이준기 씨의 부모님과 동생이 살고 있어요.

다음 주에 방학을 해요. 방학을 하면 일본에 갈 거예요.

그럼, 일본에서 만나요.

안녕히 계세요.

하즈키 드림

보고 싶은 부모님께.

Lee Joon-gi's Guide to Korea
Jeongdongjin
Where the Sun Rises on Korea

Board the night train with the person you love and see the sun rise over Jeongdongjin Beach. This is the romantic date that every Korean couple considers going on at some point or another.

Jeongdongjin Station is the train station that is closest to the ocean in South Korea. This town was named Jeongdongjin because it is located *jeongdon*—due east—of Gwanghwamun Gate in Seoul. Visiting here is like stepping into the past, and the simple, rustic buildings that greet you seem frozen in time.

Jeongdongjin is where the everyday and the romantic intersect. Each year on January 1, at around 7:40 in the morning, the sun starts to rise for the first time in the New Year. People from all over Korea gather here to make a wish as they watch the sun rise majestically above the ocean. Some people wish for luck in love, others pray that they will pass a test. And what about me? I'm hoping to get the chance to meet that special lady and live happily ever after with her, of course!

Koreans make a wish as they watch the majestic New Year sunrise.

Dreams for the Future
미래를 위한 꿈

선생님이 되고
싶어요
I Want to Be
a Teacher

Learning Objective

Situation
Dreams for the
future
Vocabulary
Jobs
Grammar
I see/indeed!
To become
Want to

ONLINE
AUDIO
00:10

벤슨 benseun	스테파니 씨, 요즘 어떻게 지내세요? **seutepani ssi, yojeum eotteoke jinaeseyo** *Stephanie, how have you been doing recently?*
스테파니 seutepani	요즘 취업 준비를 하고 있어요. **yojeum chwieop junbireul hago isseoyo** *Recently, I have been looking for a job.*
벤슨 benseun	아! 벌써 4학년이에요? 시간이 참 빠르군요! **a! beolsseo 4hangnyeonieyo? sigani cham ppareugunyo!** *Oh! Are you already in your senior year? Time really flies!*
스테파니 seutepani	네, 그래서 요즘 너무 바빠요. **ne, geuraeseo yojeum neomu bappayo** *Yeah. That's why I have been so busy lately.*
벤슨 benseun	스테파니 씨는 졸업을 하면 뭐 하고 싶으세요? **seutepani ssineun joreobeul hamyeon mwo hago sipeuseyo** *What do you want to do when you graduate?*
스테파니 seutepani	저는 시드니에 가서 한국어 선생님이 되고 싶어요. 벤슨 씨는요? **jeoneun sideunie gaseo hangugeo seonsaengnimi doego sipeoyo. benseun ssineunyo** *I want to go to Sydney and become a Korean teacher. What about you?*
벤슨 benseun	저는 예쁜 여자 친구랑 결혼하고 싶어요. **jeoneun yeppeun yeoja chingurang gyeolhonhago sipeoyo** *I want to get married to my pretty girlfriend.*
스테파니 seutepani	우아! 벤슨 씨, 여자 친구 있어요? **ua! benseun ssi, yeoja chingu isseoyo** *Wow! Benson, do you have a girlfriend?*
벤슨 benseun	아니요, 아직 없어요. 좋은 사람 있으면 소개해 주세요. **aniyo, ajik eopseoyo. joeun saram isseumyeon sogaehae juseyo** *No, I don't have one yet. If you know someone good, please introduce me.*

Vocabulary and Expressions 어휘와 표현

ONLINE AUDIO
02:20

01 직업 2 jigeop 2   Jobs 2

공무원 〔공무원〕 **gongmuwon** *government employee*

변호사 〔변호사〕 **byeonhosa** *lawyer*

회사원 〔회사원〕 **hoesawon** *office worker*   은행원 〔은행원〕 **eunhaengwon** *bank clerk*

외교관 〔외교관〕 **oegyogwan** *diplomat*   통역관 〔통역꽌〕 **tongyeokgwan** *interpreter*

작가 〔작까〕 **jakga** *writer*   시인 〔시인〕 **siin** *poet*

화가 〔화가〕 **hwaga** *painter*   피아니스트 〔피아니스트〕 **pianiseuteu** *pianist*

가수 〔가수〕 **gasu** *singer*   작사가 〔작싸가〕 **jaksaga** *lyricist*

작곡가 〔작꼭까〕 **jakgokga** *songwriter*   연예인 〔여녜인〕 **yeonyein** *celebrity*

교수 〔교수〕 **gyosu** *professor*   사업가 〔사업까〕 **saeopga** *businessperson*

디자이너 〔디자이너〕 **dijaineo** *designer*   아나운서 〔아나운서〕 **anaunseo** *news anchor*

지휘자 〔지휘자〕 **jihwija** *conductor*

영화감독 〔영화감독〕 **yeonghwagamdok** *movie director*

수의사 〔수이사〕 **suuisa** *veterinarian*   약사 〔약싸〕 **yaksa** *pharmacist*

02 한국의 회사 hangugui hoesa   Major companies in Korea

항공사 〔항공사〕 **hanggongsa** *airline*

대한항공 〔대:한항:공〕 **daehanhanggong** *Korean Air*

대기업 〔대기업〕 **daegieop** *large company, conglomerate*

삼성 〔삼성〕 **samseong** *Samsung*   LG 〔엘지〕 **LG elji** *LG*

현대 〔현대〕 **hyeondae** *Hyundai*   KT 〔케이티〕 **KT keiti** *KT*

SK 〔에스케이〕 **SK eseukei** *SK*   포스코 〔포스코〕 **poseuko** *POSCO*

방송국 〔방송국〕 **bangsongguk** *broadcasting company (radio or TV)*

KBS 〔케이비에스〕 **KBS keibieseu** *KBS*

MBC 〔엠비씨〕 **MBC embissi** *MBC*

SBS 〔에스비에스〕 **SBS eseubieseu** *SBS*

엔터테인먼트 〔엔터테임먼트〕 **enteoteinmeonteu** *talent agencies*

SM 〔에스엠〕 **SM eseuem** *SM*

YG 〔와이지〕 **YG waiji** *YG*

JYP 〔제이와이피〕 **JYP jeiwaipi** *JYP*

03 동사 dongsa   Verbs

지내다 〔지내다〕 **jinaeda** *to spend time, to be (as in the expression "how have you been")*
준비하다 〔줌ː비하다〕 **junbihada** *to prepare, to get ready*
시간이 빠르다 〔시가니빠르다〕 **sigani ppareuda** *time flies*
시작하다 〔시ː자카다〕 **sijakada** *to start*
졸업하다 〔조러파다〕 **joreopada** *to graduate (from school)*
취업하다 〔취ː어파다〕 **chwieopada** *to get a job*
사귀다 〔사귀다〕 **sagwida** *to get along with (someone)*
결혼하다 〔결혼하다〕 **gyeolhonhada** *to marry*
드럼을 치다 〔드러믈치다〕 **deureomeul chida** *to play a drum*
탈춤을 추다 〔탈추믈추다〕 **talchumeul chuda** *to perform a mask dance*

04 기타 gita   Miscellaneous

요즘 〔요즘〕 **yojeum** *lately, these days*
참 〔참〕 **cham** *really, truly*
취업 준비 〔취업준비〕 **chwieop junbi** *to look for a job*
벌써 〔벌써〕 **beolsseo** *already*
아직 〔아직〕 **ajik** *yet (as in "not yet")*
그래서 〔그래서〕 **geuraeseo** *so, for that reason*
TOPIK 시험 〔토픽시험〕 **topik siheom** *Test of Proficiency in Korean*

발음규칙 Pronunciation Rules

연음 법칙 Liaison
When a syllable with a final consonant is followed by a syllable beginning with ㅇ the final consonant is pronounced at the beginning of the second syllable in place of the ㅇ.

$$되고 \; 싶어요 \Rightarrow [되고시퍼요]$$
$$ㅍ + ㅇ \Rightarrow \emptyset + ㅍ$$

되고 싶어요 되고시퍼요 **doego sipeoyo** *I want to become*
선생님이 선생니미 **sigani** *the time is*
선생님이 **seonsaengnimi** *A teacher*
있으면 이쓰면 **isseumyeon** *if there is/are*

Grammar 문법

01 N(이) 군요 !/A- 군요 !/V- 는군요 !
N (i)gunyo!/ A-gunyo!/V-neungunyo!

I see/indeed!

Situation

This grammatical construction conveys the feeling of the sentence "Ah ha! I see!" It's generally used as a mild exclamation to show that the speaker has learned something that they didn't know before.

Explanation

These are the exclamatory expressions used to describe something that you already know or events that you have just learned about.

이준기 씨가 영화배우군요! **ijungi ssiga yeonghwabaeugunyo**
Lee Joon-gi is an actor!

시간이 참 빠르군요! **sigani cham ppareugunyo**
Time flies so fast!

오늘은 참 춥군요! **oneureun cham chupgunyo**
It is very cold today!

■ How to make N(이)군요!/A-군요!/V-는군요!

For nouns, N이군요 is used when there is a final consonant while N군요 is used when there is no final consonant. All adjectives take the form A-군요 while verbs take the form V-는군요.

Final Consonant   N + 이군요: 학생 → 학생+이군요 → 학생이군요!

A + 군요: 많다 → 많다 + 군요 → 많군요!

V + 는군요: 먹다 → 먹다 + 는군요 → 먹는군요!

No Final Consonant   N + 군요: 의사 → 의사+ 군요 → 의사군요!

A + 군요: 예쁘다 → 예쁘다 + 군요 → 예쁘군요!

V + 는군요: 가다 → 가다 + 는군요 → 가는군요!

02 N 이 / 가 되다 N i/ga doeda

To become

Situation

What will you do when you graduate? Become a singer? A teacher? Maybe a pianist? You can express these ideas by saying 가수가 되다 or 선생님이 되다 or 피아니스트가 되다.

Explanation

With the N이/가 되다 construction simply replace the N with the name of the job that you want to have. Now all that's left is making the dream come true!

리리 씨는 중국에 가면 한국어 선생님이 될 거예요.
riri ssineun jungguge gamyeon hangugeo seonsaengnimi doel geoyeyo
Lili will become a Korean language teacher when she goes back to China.

비비엔 씨는 졸업하면 통역관이 될 거예요.
bibien ssineun joreopamyeon tongyeokgwani doel geoyeyo
Vivien will become an interpreter after she graduates. [Lit., when she graduates.]

스테파니 씨는 졸업을 하면 스튜어디스가 될 거예요.
seutepani ssineun joreobeul hamyeon seutyueodiseuga doel geoyeyo
Stephanie will become a flight attendant after she graduates. [Lit., when she graduates.]

■ How to make N이/가 되다

Use N이 되다 when the noun has a final consonant and N가 되다 when it does not.

Final Consonant + 이 되다: 한국어 선생님 → 한국어 선생님이 되다.

No Final Consonant + 가 되다: 의사 → 의사가 되다.

03 V- 고 싶다 /V- 고 싶어 하다   V-go sipda/V-go sipeo hada   To want to

Situation

So you're feeling a little hungry, and there's a hamburger on the table. You think "It would be great if I could eat that burger." You say: 아! 햄버거를 먹고 싶어요.

Explanation

The construction V-고 싶다 when attached to a verb like 먹다 indicates that the subject wants the action of the verb to take place. Careful: this construction can only be used when the subject is first person (I/we) or second person (you). V-고 싶어 하다 is the appropriate construction for a third person subject.

저는 내년에 결혼하고 싶어요. jeoneun naenyeone gyeolhonhago sipeoyo
I want to get married next year.

리리 씨, 대학교를 졸업하면 뭐 하고 싶어요?
riri ssi, daehakgyoreul joreopamyeon mwo hago sipeoyo
Lili, what do you want to do after you graduate? [Lit., when you graduate?]

준이치 씨는 유명한 작곡가가 되고 싶어 해요.
junichi ssineun yumyeonghan jakgokgaga doego sipeo haeyo
Junichi wants to become a famous songwriter.

■ How to make V-고 싶다 V-고 싶어 하다

V-고 싶다 is the form that is used whether or not there is a final consonant in the last syllable of the verb stem.

Final Consonant + 고 싶다/싶어 하다:
피자를 먹다 → 피자를 먹다 + 고 싶다/싶어 하다 → 피자를 먹고 싶다/싶어 하다.

No Final Consonant + 고 싶다/싶어 하다:
영화를 보다 → 영화를 보다 + 고 싶다/싶어 하다 → 영화를 보고 싶다/싶어 하다.

활용 연습 Usage Practice

Fill in the blanks. Find the answers on page 253.

Base Form	V-고 싶다	V-고 싶어 하다
바다에 가다	바다에 가고 싶다.	바다에 가고 싶어 하다.
영화를 보다		
이준기를 만나다		
떡볶이를 먹다		
녹차를 마시다		
결혼을 하다		
가수가 되다		
스키를 타다		
태권도를 배우다		
사인을 받다		
선물을 준비하다		
휴대폰을 사다		
여자 친구를 사귀다		
삼성에 취업하다		

Conversation Practice 회화 연습

01 이것이 비빔밥이군요! **igeosi bibimbabigunyo**   **This is bibimbap!**

Use the example sentences to guide you as you practice. Find model sentences on page 253.

비빔밥

가: 이것은 비빔밥이에요.
igeoseun bibimbabieyo
This is bibimbap.

나: 아! 이것이 비빔밥이군요!
a! igeosi bibimbabigunyo
Oh! This is bibimbap!

케이크

가: 이것은 ＿＿＿＿＿＿＿＿＿＿＿＿＿＿＿ 예요/이에요.

나: 아! ＿＿＿＿＿＿＿＿＿＿＿＿＿＿＿＿!

떡

가: ＿＿＿＿＿＿＿＿＿＿＿＿＿＿＿＿＿ .

나: ＿＿＿＿＿＿＿＿＿＿＿＿＿＿＿＿＿ !

떡볶이

가: ＿＿＿＿＿＿＿＿＿＿＿＿＿＿＿＿＿ .

나: ＿＿＿＿＿＿＿＿＿＿＿＿＿＿＿＿＿ !

만들어 보세요.
슬픈 영화
화가/작가
냉면/불고기
...

가: ＿＿＿＿＿＿＿＿＿＿＿＿＿＿＿＿＿ .

나: ＿＿＿＿＿＿＿＿＿＿＿＿＿＿＿＿＿ !

02 TV를 보는군요! TVreul boneungunyo   You're watching television!

Use the example sentences to guide you as you practice. Find model sentences on page 253.

TV를 보다

가: 리리 씨, 지금 뭐 해요?
riri ssi, jigeum mwo haeyo
Lili, what are you doing now?

나: 저는 지금 TV를 봐요.
jeoneun jigeum TVreul bwayo
I am watching television now.

가: 아! TV를 보는군요!
a! TVreul boneungunyo
Oh! You're watching television!

농구를 하다

가: 벤슨 씨, _____ ?

나: 저는 지금 _____ .

가: 아! _____ !

김치를 담그다

가: 아마니 씨, _____ ?

나: _____ .

가: _____ !

만들어 보세요.

영화를 보다
친구를 만나다
수영을 하다
...

가: _____ ?

나: _____ .

가: _____ !

| 03 | 한국어 선생님이 될 거예요 .
hangugeo seonsaengnimi doel geoyeyo | I'm going to become
a Korean teacher |

Use the example sentences to guide you as you practice. Find model sentences on page 253.

의사

가: 리리 씨, 졸업을 하면 뭐 할 거예요?
riri ssi, joreobeul hamyeon mwo hal geoyeyo
Lili, what are you going to do after you graduate? [Lit., when you graduate?]

나: 저는 졸업을 하면 의사가 될 거예요.
jeoneun joreobeul hamyeon uisaga doel geoyeyo
I'm going to be a doctor after I graduate. [Lit. when I graduate.]

경찰관

가: 벤슨 씨, _____?

나: 저는 _____ .

통역관

가: 비비엔 씨, _____?

나: _____ .

아나운서

가: 아마니 씨, _____?

나: _____ .

요리사

가: 퍼디 씨, _____?

나: 저는 _____ .

한국어
선생님

가: 스테파니 씨, _____?

나: _____.

만들어 보세요.

가: _____?

나: _____.

스튜어디스

음악가

예

수의사

회사원

우체부

약사

04 저는 바다에 가고 싶어요.   jeoneun badae gago sipeoyo   **I want to go to the beach**

Use the example sentences to guide you as you practice. Find model sentences on page 253.

가: 최지영 씨, 뭐 하고 싶어요?
choejiyeong ssi, mwo hago sipeoyo
Jiyoung, what do you want to do?

나: 저는 바다에 가고 싶어요.
jeoneun badae gago sipeoyo
I want to go to the beach.

가: 최지영 씨는 바다에 가고 싶어 해요.
choejiyeong ssineun badae gago sipeo haeyo
Jiyoung wants to go to the beach.

커피를 마시다

가: 리리 씨, _____?

나: 저는 _____.

가: 리리 씨는, _____.

요리를 하다

가: 퍼디 씨, _____?

나: _____.

가: _____.

드럼을 치다

가: 이준기 씨, _____?

나: _____.

가: _____.

콘서트에 가다

가: 하즈키 씨, _____?

나: _____.

가: _____.

만들어 보세요.

가: _____?

나: _____.

가: _____.

예

스키를 타다

탈춤을 추다

번지 점프를 하다

*〈칭찬해줘〉를 부르다

빵을 먹다

* 칭찬해줘 (English title "Sweet Memory")
was a song released by Lee Joon-gi.

Listening Practice 듣기 연습

ONLINE AUDIO
05:41

Read the two questions below and then listen to the online audio file to find the answers, choosing from the illustrations. You can find the audio script on page 240.

문제 1 그림에서 스테파니 씨가 시험이 끝나면 하고 싶은 것을 모두 고르세요.

문제 2 그림에서 스테파니 씨가 졸업을 하면 하고 싶은 것을 모두 고르세요.

Talking with Lee Joon-gi   이준기와 이야기하기

ONLINE AUDIO
07:44

Try having a conversation with Lee Joon-gi as you listen to the audio. You can find a translation of this conversation on page 246.

이준기	아마니 씨, 요즘 어떻게 지내세요?
아마니	저는 요즘 TOPIK 공부를 하고 있어요.
이준기	아, 그렇군요! 다음 주가 시험이군요!
아마니	네, 그래서 요즘 너무 바빠요.
이준기	아마니 씨는 졸업을 하면 뭐 하고 싶으세요?
아마니	저는 사우디에 가서 아나운서가 되고 싶어요.
이준기	아, 그렇군요!
아마니	이준기 씨는 졸업을 하면 뭐 하고 싶으세요?
이준기	저는 예쁜 여자 친구랑 결혼하고 싶어요.
아마니	우아! 이준기 씨 여자 친구 있어요?
이준기	아니요, 아직 없어요. 좋은 사람 있으면 소개해 주세요.

연습해 보기 Let's Practice

Use the example sentences to guide you as you practice. It's even more helpful to do this with a friend who is studying Korean.

최지영   리리 씨, 오늘 오후에 뭐 하고 싶어요?

리리   저는 오후에 영화를 보고 싶어요.

질문 친구	1) 리리	2)	3)
오늘 오후/뭐 하다?	영화를 보다		
이번 주말/뭐 하다?	바다에 가다		
지금 누구를 만나다?	친구를 만나다		
졸업하면 뭐 하다?	취직하다		
이준기 씨를 만나면 뭐 하다?	<칭찬해줘>를 함께 부르다		

 Introduce your friends just as Jiyoung does.

최지영   리리 씨는 오늘 오후에 영화를 보고 싶어 해요.
          이번 주말에 바다에 가고 싶어 해요.
          지금 친구를 만나고 싶어 하고, 졸업하면 취직하고 싶어 해요.
          그리고 이준기 씨를 만나면 <칭찬해줘>를 함께 부르고 싶어 해요.

Lee Joon-gi's Guide to Korea

Namwon

City that is Home to a Famous Love Story

The city of Namwon is the setting for *The Story of Chunhyang*, the classic Korean romance. If *Romeo and Juliet* is the iconic tragic love story, *The Story of Chunhyang* is the ultimate tale of lovers who must overcome great difficulties to achieve happiness.

The story when a young man called Mongryong sees Chunhyang on a swing and falls head over heels in love with her. After he finally professes his love to her, they make their wedding vows . . . but not long after that Mongryong has to leave Namwon to go to Hanyang (the old name for Seoul) so he can take the government entrance exam. After he leaves, the new magistrate in Namwon is attracted to Chunhyang. When she refuses his advances, he throws her in prison. Meanwhile in Hanyang, Mongryong passes the exam and is appointed as a secret royal inspector, who investigates local magistrates. He returns to Namwon, rescues Chunhyang, and they are reunited. Each year, the city organizes the Namwon Chunhyang Festival to celebrate the love of Chunhyang and Mongryong. Scattered across the town are tantalizing traces of the lovers, leading one to wonder if the story might be more than fiction. You know, I'm getting the urge to try playing Mongryong myself. How do you think I would do?

Mongryong returned home after passing the government entrance exam and becoming a royal inspector.

Chunhyang and Mongryong overcame all kinds of difficulties and finally got married.

함께 떠나요!

Asking for Directions
길 묻기

교보문고가
어디예요?
Where is
Kyobo
Bookstore?

Learning Objective

Situation
Asking for directions
Vocabulary
Streets
Locations
Directions
Grammar
In the middle of
doing something
Directions
About/approximately

ONLINE
AUDIO
00:10

리리 riri	실례합니다. 교보문고가 어디예요? **sillyehamnida. gyobomungoga eodiyeyo** *Excuse me. Where is Kyobo Bookstore?*
이준기 ijungi	이 길로 똑바로 가다가 두 번째 신호등에서 왼쪽으로 가세요. **i gillo ttokbaro gadaga du beonjjae sinhodeungeseo oenjjogeuro gaseyo** *Go straight on this road and turn left at the second traffic light.*
리리 riri	두 번째 신호등에서 왼쪽으로 가면 바로 보여요? **du beonjjae sinhodeungeseo oenjjogeuro gamyeon baro boyeoyo** *Will I see it as soon as I turn left at the second traffic light?*
이준기 ijungi	왼쪽으로 돌아서 50미터 정도 가면 교보빌딩이 보여요. **oenjjogeuro doraseo 50miteo jeongdo gamyeon gyobobildingi boyeoyo** *If you turn left and go for about 50 meters, you will see the Kyobo Building.* 교보문고는 교보빌딩 지하 1층에 있어요. **gyobomungoneun gyobobilding jiha 1cheunge isseoyo** *Kyobo Bookstore is on basement level 1 in the Kyobo Building.*
리리 riri	여기서 걸어서 얼마나 걸려요? **yeogiseo georeoseo eolmana geollyeoyo** *How long will it take to walk from here?*
이준기 ijungi	걸어서 10분쯤 걸려요. **georeoseo 10 (sip) bunjjeum geollyeoyo** *It will take about 10 minutes on foot.*
리리 riri	네, 알겠습니다. 감사합니다. **ne, algetseumnida. gamsahamnida** *OK. Thanks.*

Vocabulary and Expressions 어휘와 표현

ONLINE AUDIO
01:55

01 길 gil — Street

사거리 〔사거리〕 **sageori** *4-way intersection*
육교 〔육꾜〕 **yukgyo** *pedestrian bridge*
신호등 〔신호등〕 **sinhodeung** *traffic light*
대각선 〔대각썬〕 **daegakseon** *diagonal line*
인도 〔인도〕 **indo** *sidewalk*
골목 〔골목〕 **golmok** *alley*

횡단보도 〔횡담보도〕 **hoengdanbodo** *crosswalk*
지하도 〔지하도〕 **jihado** *underground walkway*
표지판 〔표지판〕 **pyojipan** *street sign*
맞은편 〔마즌편〕 **majeunpyeon** *opposite side*
중앙선 〔중앙선〕 **jungangseon** *center line*

02 위치 wichi — Location

앞 〔압〕 **ap** *in front of*
오른쪽 〔오른쪽〕 **oreunjjok** *the right side*
똑바로 〔똑빠로〕 **ttokbaro** *straight ahead, correctly*
곧장 〔곧짱〕 **gotjang** *straight ahead, right away*
쭉 〔쭉〕 **jjuk** *straight ahead*

뒤 〔뒤〕 **dwi** *behind*
왼쪽 〔왼쪽〕 **oenjjok** *the left side*

03 N 째 N jjae — Ordinal numbers

첫 번째 〔첟뻔째〕 **cheot beonjjae** *first*
두 번째 〔두번째〕 **du beonjjae** *second*
세 번째 〔세번째〕 **se beonjjae** *third*
네 번째 〔네번째〕 **ne beonjjae** *fourth*
다섯 번째 〔다섣뻔째〕 **daseot beonjjae** *fifth*
여섯 번째 〔여섣뻔째〕 **yeoseot beonjjae** *sixth*
일곱 번째 〔일곱뻔째〕 **ilgop beonjjae** *seventh*
여덟 번째 〔여덜번째〕 **yeodeol beonjjae** *eighth*
아홉 번째 〔아홉뻔째〕 **ahop beonjjae** *ninth*
열 번째 〔열번째〕 **yeol beonjjae** *tenth*
스무 번째 〔스무번째〕 **seumu beonjjae** *twentieth*
서른 번째 〔서른번째〕 **seoreun beonjjae** *thirtieth*
백 번째 〔백뻔째〕 **baek beonjjae** *hundredth*
천 번째 〔천번째〕 **cheon beonjjae** *thousandth*

04 동사 dongsa   Verbs

돌다 〔돌다〕 **dolda** *to turn*

걸리다 〔걸리다〕 **geollida** *to take (a certain amount of time)*

건너다 〔건너다〕 **geonneoda** *to cross*

울다 〔울다〕 **ulda** *to cry*

깨다 〔깨다〕 **kkaeda** *to break, to wake up*

보이다 〔보이다〕 **boida** *to be seen*

걷다 〔걷따〕 **geotda** *to walk*

놀라다 〔놀라다〕 **nollada** *to be surprised*

싸우다 〔싸우다〕 **ssauda** *to fight*

05 기타 gita   Miscellaneous

*교보문고 〔교보뭉고〕 **gyobomungo** *Kyobo Bookstore*

교보빌딩 〔교보빌딩〕 **gyobobilding** *Kyobo Building*

풍선 〔풍선〕 **pungseon** *balloon*

하늘 〔하늘〕 **haneul** *sky*

택시 승강장 〔택씨승강장〕 **taeksi seunggangjang** *taxi stand*

지하철역 〔지하철력〕 **jihacheollyeok** *subway station*

버스정류장 〔버스정뉴장〕 **beoseujeongnyujang** *bus stop*

정도 〔정도〕 **jeongdo** *about, approximately*

*Kyobo Books was built on the philosophy of the bookstore's founder, the late Sin Yong-ho, which was that "people make books, and books make people." Since the early 1980s, when it first opened for business in Gwanghwamun, it has become Korea's representative bookstore, providing Koreans with "food for the soul."

발음규칙 Pronunciation Rules

경음화 Tensification

When the final consonant of syllable is ㄱ, ㄷ, ㅂ and the initial sound of the next syllable is ㄱ, ㄷ, ㅂ, ㅅ, or ㅈ change to ㄲ, ㄸ, ㅃ, ㅆ, and ㅉ.

$$똑바로 ⇒ 〔똑빠로〕$$

$$ㄱ + ㅂ ⇒ ㄱ + ㅃ$$

똑바로 똑빠로 **ttokbaro** *straight ahead*

육교 육꾜 **yukgyo** *pedestrian bridge*

알겠습니다 알겓씀니다 **algetseumnida** *I understand.*

대각선 대각썬 **daegakseon** *diagonal line*

Grammar 문법

01 V- 다가 V-daga
In the middle of doing something

Situation

You went to the bathroom before you'd finished your coffee. You say: 저는 커피를 마시다가 화장실에 갔어요. You were on your way home when you met a friend. You say: 저는 집에 가다가 친구를 만났어요.

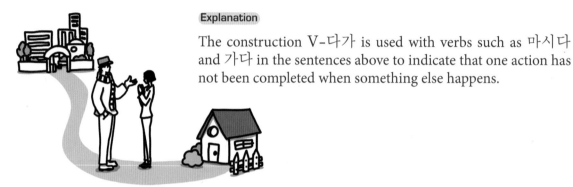

Explanation

The construction V-다가 is used with verbs such as 마시다 and 가다 in the sentences above to indicate that one action has not been completed when something else happens.

리리 씨는 집에 가다가 친구를 만났어요.
riri ssineun jibe gadaga chingureul mannasseoyo
Lili met her friend on her way home.

책을 읽다가 잤어요.
chaegeul ikdaga jasseoyo
(I) fell asleep while reading a book.

커피를 마시다가 화장실에 갔어요.
keopireul masidaga hwajangsire gasseoyo
(I) was drinking coffee, and (I) went to the toilet.

영화를 보다가 울었어요.
yeonghwareul bodaga ureosseoyo
(I) cried while watching the movie.

■ **How to make** V-다가

V-다가 is the form that is used whether or not there is a final consonant in the last syllable of the verb stem.

Final Consonant + 다가: 먹다 → 먹다 + 다가 → 먹다가

No Final Consonant + 다가: 보다 → 보다 + 다가 → 보다가

활용 연습 Usage Practice

Fill in the blanks. Find the answers on page 253.

Base Form	V-다가 V-았/었어요
집에 가다/친구를 만나다	집에 가다가 친구를 만났어요.
밥을 먹다/전화를 하다	
남자 친구와 싸우다/울다	
책을 읽다/자다	
숙제를 하다/편지를 쓰다	
술을 마시다/노래를 하다	
영화를 보다/친구를 생각하다	
도서관에 가다/커피를 사다	
잠을 자다/놀라서 깨다	

02 N(으)로 N(eu)ro

In a direction

Situation

We often use words of direction such as 오른쪽 or 왼쪽 or 위 or 아래 to tell someone which direction to go. For example, we can say: 오른쪽으로 [위로, 아래로] 가세요. Another use of this particle is with words that express a method of doing something such as 볼펜 and 지하철. We can apply it in phrases such as 볼펜으로 써요 and 지하철로 가요.

Explanation

N(으)로 is used in two situations: when indicating a direction as with 오른쪽으로 or 위로, and when indicating the method by which something is done as with 볼펜으로 or 지하철로.

똑바로 가다가 왼쪽으로 가세요.
ttokbaro gadaga oenjjogeuro gaseyo
Please go straight, then turn left.

풍선이 하늘로 올라갔어요.
pungseoni haneullo ollagasseoyo
The balloon went up in the sky.

지하철로 20분 걸려요.
jihacheollo 20 (isip) bun geollyeoyo
It takes about twenty minutes by subway.

■ **How to make N(으)로**

If there is a final consonant in the last syllable of a noun, use N 으로; if there is no final consonant or if the final consonant is ㄹ, use N 로.

Final Consonant + 으로: 왼쪽 → 왼쪽으로, 숟가락 → 숟가락으로

No Final Consonant + 로: 아래 → 아래로, 버스 → 버스로

Final Consonant ㄹ + 로: 하늘 → 하늘로, 지하철 → 지하철로

03 N 쯤 N jjeum

About/approximately

You think it probably takes one hour and twenty or thirty minutes to fly from Korea to Japan. You say: 한국에서 일본까지 1시간 30분쯤 걸려요. You walk home from school. It probably takes 15, 20, or 30 minutes, but you don't know for sure. You say: 20분쯤 걸려요.

Explanation

The construction N쯤 is used to express an approximate amount of time. Just insert a noun of time such as 1시간 or 하루 in the N slot. Some corresponding English expressions for N쯤 are "around N" and "about N."

집에서 학교까지 걸어서 20분쯤 걸려요.
jibeseo hakgyokkaji georeoseo 20 (isip) bunjjeum geollyeoyo
It takes me about twenty minutes to walk from home to school.

서울에서 부산까지 다섯 시간쯤 걸려요.
seoureseo busankkaji daseot siganjjeum geollyeoyo
It takes about five hours from Seoul to Busan.

한국에서 프랑스까지 하루쯤 걸려요.
hangugeseo peurangseukkaji harujjeum geollyeoyo
It takes about one day from Korea to France.

■ How to make N쯤

Whether or not there is a final consonant in the last syllable of the noun, simply use the form N쯤.

Final Consonant + 쯤: 한 시간 → 한 시간쯤

No Final Consonant + 쯤: 하루 → 하루쯤

Conversation Practice 회화 연습

01 오른쪽으로 가세요. oreunjjogeuro gaseyo   **Please turn right.**

Use the example sentences to guide you as you practice. Find model sentences on page 253.

화장실, 오른쪽

가: 실례지만, 화장실이 어디예요?
sillyejiman, hwajangsiri eodiyeyo
Excuse me, where is the toilet?

나: 화장실은 오른쪽으로 가세요.
hwajangsireun oreunjjogeuro gaseyo
Please turn right.

사무실, 왼쪽

가: 실례지만, _____?

나: _____.

광화문, 저쪽

가: _____, _____?

나: _____.

우체국, 옆

가: _____, _____?

나: _____.

만들어 보세요.
도서관/아래
영화관/앞
수영장/위
…

가: _____?

나: _____.

02 버스로 30 분쯤 걸려요 .
beoseuro 30 (samsip) bunjjeum geollyeoyo
It takes about thirty minutes by bus.

Use the example sentences to guide you as you practice. Find model sentences on page 254.

강남→광화문
버스/30분

가: 강남에서 광화문까지 얼마나 걸려요?
gangnameseo gwanghwamunkkaji eolmana geollyeoyo
How long does it take from Gangnam to Gwanghwamun?

나: 광화문까지 버스로 30분쯤 걸려요.
gwanghwamunkkaji beoseuro 30 (samsip) bunjjeum geollyeyo
It takes about thirty minutes to Gwanghwamun by bus.

한국→일본
비행기/2시간

가: _____ ?

나: _____ .

한국→스페인
배/2달

가: _____ ?

나: _____ .

집→명동
걸어서 20분

가: _____ ?

나: _____ .

만들어 보세요.

서울→베이징
비행기/3시간

학교→집
걸어서 15분
…

가: _____ ?

나: _____ .

03 똑바로 가다가 신호등에서 왼쪽으로 가세요 .
ttokbaro gadaga sinhodeungeseo oenjjogeuro gaseyo

Please go straight, then turn left at the traffic light.

Use the example sentences to guide you as you practice. Find model sentences on page 254.

똑바로 가다
신호등에서 왼쪽으로 가다

가: 실례지만, 우리병원이 어디예요?
sillyejiman, uribyeongwoni eodiyeyo
Excuse me, where is Uri hospital?

나: 똑바로 가다가 신호등에서 왼쪽으로 가세요 .
ttokbaro gadaga sinhodeungeseo oenjjogeuro gaseyo
Please go straight, then turn left at the traffic light.

오른쪽으로 가다
사거리에서 왼쪽으로 가다

가: 실례지만 _____ 이 어디예요?

나: _____ .

옆길로 가다
육교를 건너다

가: _____ , _____ ?

나: _____ .

사거리에서 왼쪽으로 가다
아래로 50m쯤 가다

가: _____ , _____ ?

나: _____ .

은행 옆길로 가다
육교를 건너다

가: _____ , _____ ?

나: _____ .

뒤로 돌아서
100m쯤 가다/왼쪽

한국대학교

가: _____ , _____ ?

나: _____ .

이쪽으로 쭉 가다
오른쪽

국회의사당

가: _____ , _____ ?

나: _____ .

만들어 보세요.

가: _____ ?

나: _____ .

예

광화문
왼쪽으로 가다
사거리에서
길을 건너다

청와대
위로
100m쯤 가다
횡단보도를 건너다

극장
앞으로 곧장 가다
편의점에서
오른쪽으로 가다

04 인사동에 가다가 이준기 씨를 만났어요.
insadonge gadaga ijungi ssireul mannasseoyo

I met Joon-gi on the way to Insadong.

Use the example sentences to guide you as you practice. Find model sentences on page 254.

가: 스테파니 씨, 어제 뭐 했어요?
seutepani ssi, eoje mwo haesseoyo
Stephanie, what did you do yesterday?

나: 인사동에 가다가 이준기 씨를 만났어요.
insadonge gadaga ijungi ssireul mannasseoyo
I met Joon-gi on the way to Insadong.

가: 준이치 씨, _____?

나: _____.

가: 하즈키 씨, _____?

나: _____.

가: 비비엔 씨, _____?

나: _____.

가: 아마니 씨, _____?

나: _____.

음악을 듣다
자다

가: 앙리 씨, _____?

나: _____.

술을 마시다
노래하다

가: 벤슨 씨, _____?

나: _____.

만들어 보세요.

가: _____?

나: _____.

예)

TV를 보다
전화를 받다

길을 가다
넘어지다

만화를 읽다
웃다

Listening Practice 1 듣기 연습 1

ONLINE AUDIO
05:03

Read the question below the map, listen to the conversation and mark on the map the location of the place. You can find the audio script on page 240.

문제 지하철역은 어디에 있어요? 그림에 표시하세요.

Listening Practice 2 듣기 연습 2

ONLINE AUDIO
06:27

Read the question below the map, listen to the conversation and mark on the map the location of the place. You can find the audio script on page 240.

문제 커피숍은 어디에 있어요? 그림에 표시하세요.

Talking with Lee Joon-gi   이준기와 이야기하기

ONLINE AUDIO
07:38

Try having a conversation with Lee Joon-gi as you listen to the audio. You can find a translation of this conversation on page 246.

하즈키	실례지만 병원이 어디에 있어요?
이준기	이 길로 똑바로 가다가 두 번째 신호등에서 왼쪽으로 가세요.
하즈키	두 번째 신호등에서 왼쪽으로 가면 바로 보여요?
이준기	왼쪽으로 돌아서 똑바로 가면 은행이 있어요. 은행 옆길로 쭉 가면 행복빌딩이 보여요. 병원은 행복빌딩 3층에 있어요.
하즈키	여기서 걸어서 얼마나 걸려요?
이준기	걸어서 15분쯤 걸려요.
하즈키	네 알겠습니다. 감사합니다.

연습해 보기 Let's Practice

Interview up to three people, using the example sentences below. If you don't have any Korean speakers to interview, you can make up your own responses.

최지영	스테파니 씨 주말에 뭐 했어요?
스테파니	영화를 보다가 잤어요.

최지영	준이치 씨 주말에 뭐 했어요?
준이치	드라마를 보다가 운동을 했어요.

친구 \ 질문	1) 리리
1) 스테파니	영화를 보다가 잤어요.
2) 준이치	드라마를 보다가 운동을 했어요.
3)	
4)	
5)	

 Introduce your friends just as Jiyoung does.

최지영	스테파니 씨는 주말에 영화를 보다가 잤어요.
	준이치 씨는 주말에 드라마를 보다가 운동을 했어요.

Lee Joon-gi's Guide to Korea

Gwangju

City of Peace and Democracy

The name Gwangju evokes memories of a difficult episode in contemporary Korean history. In May 1980, the citizens of Gwangju stood up to the military dictatorship in the hopes of achieving democracy, and many of them lost their lives in the resulting conflict. This tragic episode is referred to as the Gwangju Democratization Movement.

Many people who visit Gwangju pay their respects at the National May 18 Democratic Cemetery, where those who died in the conflict are buried, and reflect on the sadness of that day. Even today, various records that shed light on the horrible events that transpired can be found throughout the city. These documents have been selected for inclusion on the UNESCO Memory of the World Register, indicating their value as a common heritage for us all. I hope we will soon see the last of such bloody struggles—not only in Korea, but throughout the world.

These records are a lasting testament to the terrible tragedy of that day.

Taking a Taxi
택시에 타서

Learning Objective

Situation
Taking a taxi
Vocabulary
Transportation
Traffic
Grammar
Polite requests
Giving a reason
Within/in

ONLINE
AUDIO
00:10

기사 gisa	어서 오세요. 손님, 어디로 갈까요?
	eoseo oseyo. sonnim, eodiro galkkayo
	Please get in. Where would you like to go?

하즈키 hajeuki	인사동으로 가 주세요.
	insadongeuro ga juseyo
	Please take me to Insadong.

기사 gisa	네, 알겠습니다.
	ne, algetseumnida
	Alright.

하즈키 hajeuki	여기에서 인사동까지 얼마나 걸려요?
	yeogieseo insadongkkaji eolmana geollyeoyo
	How long does it take to get from here to Insadong?

기사 gisa	이 시간대에는 길이 막히지 않을 테니까 30분 안에 도착할 거예요.
	i sigandaeeneun giri makiji aneul tenikka 30 (samsip) bun ane dochakal geoyeyo
	At this time of day, traffic should be light, so we'll probably arrive in 30 minutes.

하즈키 hajeuki	네.
	ne
	OK.

기사 gisa	저기 보이는 사거리에서 어디로 갈까요?
	jeogi boineun sageorieseo eodiro galkkayo
	Where would you like to go from the intersection over there?

(continues overleaf)

하즈키 　사거리에서 우회전하세요.
hajeuki **sageorieseo uhoejeonhaseyo**
Make a right turn at the intersection.
우회전하면 바로 횡단보도가 있어요.
uhoejeonhamyeon baro hoengdanbodoga isseoyo
As soon as you turn right there will be a crosswalk.
그 근처에 세워 주세요.
geu geuncheoe sewo juseyo
Please stop around there.

기사 　네, 알겠습니다. 어디쯤에 세워 드릴까요?
gisa **ne, algetseumnida. eodijjeume sewo deurilkkayo**
OK. Where would you like me to stop?

하즈키 　저기 보이는 하얀 건물 앞에 세워 주세요. 얼마예요?
hajeuki **jeogi boineun hayan geonmul ape sewo juseyo. eolmayeyo**
Please stop in front of that white building over there. How much is it?

기사 　만이천 원입니다.
gisa **manicheon wonimnida**
12,000 won.

하즈키 　여기 있습니다. 감사합니다.
hajeuki **yeogi itseumnida. gamsahamnida**
Here you go. Thank you.

기사 　감사합니다. 안녕히 가세요.
gisa **gamsahamnida. annyeonghi gaseyo**
Thanks. Goodbye.

Vocabulary and Expressions 어휘와 표현

ONLINE AUDIO
02:44

---

01 동사 dongsa   **Verbs**

막히다 〔마키다〕 **makida** *to be blocked (often used for bad traffic)*
출발하다 〔출발하다〕 **chulbalhada** *to set out, to depart*
도착하다 〔도차카다〕 **dochakada** *to arrive*
세우다 〔세우다〕 **seuda** *to stop (a car)*

---

02 길 gil   **On the road**

우회전하다 〔우회전하다〕 **uhoejeonhada** *to turn right*
좌회전하다 〔좌회전하다〕 **jwahoejeonhada** *to turn left*
직진하다 〔직찐하다〕 **jikjinhada** *to go straight*
유턴하다 〔유턴하다〕 **yuteonhada** *to make a U-turn*

---

03 기타 gita   **Miscellaneous**

어서 오세요 〔어서오세요〕 **eoseo oseyo** *Please come in*
알겠습니다 〔알겓씀니다〕 **algetseumnida** *I understand, OK, alright*
근처 〔근처〕 **geuncheo** *the area, the vicinity*
걱정하다 〔걱쩡하다〕 **geokjeonghada** *to worry*

발음규칙 Pronunciation Rules

'ㅎ' 탈락 Silent ㅎ
The final consonant ㅎ is silent when it precedes a conjugative ending that starts with ㅇ such as 아, 어 or 으.

$$\text{않을 테니까} \Rightarrow [\text{아늘테니까}]$$
$$\text{ㅎ} + \text{을} \Rightarrow \varnothing + \text{을}$$

좋은 조은 **joeun** *good*
좋아요 조아요 **joayo** *(It) is good*
많이 마니 **mani** *a lot*
~않아요 ~아나요 **anayo** *is/am/are not, do(es) not*

Grammar 문법

01 V-/어 주세요 V-a/eo juseyo   Polite requests

Situation

You want Lili to give you the coffee she's bought. You say: 리리 씨, 커피를 사 주세요. You want the taxi driver to take you to Insadong. You say: 인사동으로 가 주세요.

Explanation

With the V-아/어 주세요 construction, we can ask other people to do the actions represented by verbs such as 사다 and 가다. The construction is not compatible with things that have already been done or are being done right now. In English, this can be expressed by adding "please" before the verb, though "me" may need to be added depending on the situation ("please buy me a book," for example).

리리 씨, 피아노를 쳐 주세요.
riri ssi, pianoreul chyeo juseyo
Lili, play the piano, please.

아저씨, 남산으로 가 주세요.
ajeossi, namsaneuro ga juseyo
Sir, take me to Namsan Mountain, please.

은행 앞에서 세워 주세요.
eunhaeng apeseo sewo juseyo
Stop (the taxi) in front of the bank, please.

■ How to make V-아/어 주세요

When the vowels ㅏ or ㅗ appear in the final syllable of the verb stem, use V-아 주세요. When these vowels are not present, use V-어 주세요.

ㅏ, ㅗ일 때 + 아 주세요: 일어나다 → 일어나다 + 아 주세요 → 일어나 주세요

ㅏ, ㅗ가 아닐 때 + 어 주세요: 읽다 → 읽다 + 어 주세요 → 읽어 주세요

~하다일 때 → ~해 주세요: 청소하다 → 청소하다 + 해 주세요 → 청소해 주세요

Final Consonant ㄷ → ㄹ + 어 주세요: 듣다 → 듣다 + ㄹ어 주세요 → 들어 주세요

Final Consonant ㅂ → 우 + 어 주세요: 줍다 → 줍다 + 워(우 + 어) 주세요 → 주워 주세요

02 A/V-(으)ㄹ 테니까 A/V-(eu)r tenikka **Giving a reason**

Situation

You're going to study and you want people to be quiet. You say: 저는 공부를 할 테니까 조용히 해 주세요. You want to encourage someone to study hard, since the test will probably be difficult. In this situation, you can say, 시험이 어려울 테니까 열심히 하세요.

Explanation

The grammatical construction A/V-(으)ㄹ 테니까 combines verbs like 공부하다 with adjectives like 어렵다. This allows you to join two sentences in the format of 그 [verb/adjective] 를 할 거예요. 그러니까 into one. The first clause of A/V-(으)ㄹ 테니까 must refer to something that will happen in the future (tomorrow, this weekend, next month, next year, etc). Don't use it to talk about things you have already done or are doing right now.

길이 막힐 테니까 일찍 오세요.
giri makil tenikka iljjik oseyo
Please come early because there will be traffic jams.

주말에 올 테니까 걱정하지 마세요.
jumare ol tenikka geokjeonghaji maseyo
Please don't worry because I will come at the weekend.

비비엔 씨가 바쁠 테니까 나중에 전화하세요.
bibien ssiga bappeul tenikka najunge jeonhwahaseyo
Please call Vivien later because she is busy.

■ How to make A/V- (으)ㄹ테니까

If there is a final consonant in the last syllable of the verb, use V-을 테니까; if there is no final consonant or if the final consonant is ㄹ, use V-ㄹ 테니까.

Final Consonant + 을 테니까: 먹다 → 먹다 +을 테니까 → 먹을 테니까

No Final Consonant + ㄹ 테니까 : 만나다 → 만나다 +ㄹ 테니까 → 만날 테니까

Final Consonant ㄹ → ㄹ + ㄹ 테니까: 만들다 → 만들다 + ㄹ 테니까 → 만들 테니까

Final Consonant ㄷ → ㄹ + 을 테니까: 듣다 → 듣다 + ㄹ을 테니까 → 들을 테니까

Final Consonant ㅂ → 우 + ㄹ 테니까: 어렵다 → 어렵다 + 울(우 + ㄹ) 테니까 → 어려울 테니까

활용 연습 Usage Practice

Fill in the blanks. Find the answers on page 254.

Base Form	V-아/어 주세요	Base Form	A/V-(으)ㄹ 테니까
세우다	세워 주세요.	덥다	
열다		춥다	추울 테니까
닫다		바쁘다	
만들다		청소하다	
출발하다		차가 막히다	
듣다		앉다	
입다		멀다	

03 N 안에 N ane

In/within

Situation

You're working now and will probably be finished in an hour.
You say: 이 일이 한 시간 안에 끝날 거예요. It is 2 o'clock.
You are cleaning. You'll probably be finished before 3 o'clock.
What you say: 청소가 한 시간 안에 끝날 거예요.

Explanation

In the N 안에 construction, nouns such as 한 시간 and 한 달 which
express an amount of time go into the N slot. The construction means
"before the time that the noun represents has passed." In English, the
preposition "in" is used in a very similar way, as in the sentence "I will be
there in an hour."

10분 안에 도착해요.
10 (sip) bun ane dochakaeyo
(I) will be arriving in 10 minutes.

이 일은 한 시간 안에 할 수 있어요.
i ireun han sigan ane hal su isseoyo
I can finish the work in an hour.

집에서 회사까지 걸어서 20분 안에 갈 수 있어요.
jibeseo hoesakkaji georeoseo 20 (isip) bun ane gal su isseoyo
I can get from home to the office in twenty minutes.

■ How to make N 안에

Use N안에 whether or not there is a final consonant in the last syllable of the noun.

Final Consonant + 안에: 한 시간 → 한 시간 안에

No Final Consonant + 안에 : 이번 주 → 이번 주 안에

Conversation Practice 회화 연습

01 인사동으로 가 주세요.   **insadongeuro ga juseyo**   **Take me to Insadong, please.**

Use the example sentences to guide you as you practice. Find model sentences on page 254.

인사동

가: 손님, 어디로 갈까요?
sonnim, eodiro galkkayo
Madam/Sir, where do you want to go?

나: 인사동으로 가 주세요.
insadongeuro ga juseyo
Take me to Insadong, please.

한국대학교

가: 손님, _____ ?

나: _____ .

우리병원

우리 ✚ 병원

가: _____ , _____ ?

나: _____ .

교보문고

가: _____ , _____ ?

나: _____ .

만들어 보세요.

홍대
대학로
강남역
...

가: _____ ?

나: _____ .

| 02 | 스타벅스 앞에서 세워 주세요 .
seutabeokseu apeseo sewo juseyo | **Stop (the taxi) in front of Starbucks,
please.** |

Use the example sentences to guide you as you practice. Find model sentences on page 254.

스타벅스 앞

가: 손님, 어디에 세워 드릴까요?
sonnim, eodie sewo deurilkkayo
Madam/Sir, where do you want me to stop?

나: 스타벅스 앞에서 세워 주세요.
seutabeokseu apeseo sewo juseyo
Stop (the taxi) in front of Starbucks, please.

지하철역 근처

가: 손님, _____ ?

나: _____ .

주유소 앞

가: _____ , _____ ?

나: _____ .

횡단보도 근처

가: _____ , _____ ?

나: _____ .

만들어 보세요.
하얀 건물 앞
도서관 옆
지하도 근처
...

가: _____ ?

나: _____ .

111

03 갈 테니까 기다리세요. gal tenikka gidariseyo **Please wait because I am coming.**

Use the example sentences to guide you as you practice. Find model sentences on page 254.

갈 테니까 기다리세요.
gal tenikka gidariseyo
Please wait because I am coming.

바쁠 테니까 오지 마세요.
bappeul tenikka oji maseyo
Please don't come because you will be busy.

_____.

_____.

_____.

_____.

우산을 빌려 주다
걱정하다 X

_____ .

빌려 주다
사다 X

_____ .

만들어 보세요.

_____ .

Listening Practice 1 듣기 연습 1

ONLINE AUDIO
04:18

Listen to the dialogues and write down where the people are going. You can find the audio script on page 240.

문제 이 사람들은 어디에 가는지 써 보세요.

1) 리리: _____   2) 비비엔: _____

Listening Practice 2 듣기 연습 2

ONLINE AUDIO
06:05

Listen to the dialogues and write down where the people get out of the taxi. You can find the audio script on page 240.

문제 이 사람들은 어디에서 내리는지 써 보세요.

1) 퍼디: _____   2) 벤슨: _____

Talking with Lee Joon-gi 이준기와 이야기하기

ONLINE AUDIO
07:25

Try having a conversation with Lee Joon-gi as you listen to the audio. You can find a translation of this conversation on page 246.

기사	어서 오세요. 손님, 어디로 갈까요?
이준기	여의도로 가 주세요.
기사	네, 알겠습니다.
이준기	여기에서 여의도까지 얼마나 걸려요?
기사	길이 막히면 한 시간쯤 걸려요. 이 시간에는 길이 막히지 않을 테니까 40분 안에 도착할 거예요.
이준기	네.
기사	아이고, 퇴근 시간이라서 길이 많이 막히는군요!
이준기	좀 더 빠른 길은 없어요?
기사	조금 돌아가는 길이 있어요. 아마 이 길보다는 빠를 겁니다.
이준기	그럼, 빠른 길로 가 주세요.
기사	네, 알겠습니다. 저기 보이는 사거리에서 우회전할까요?
이준기	네, 우회전하면 바로 횡단보도가 보일 거예요. 그 앞에 세워 주세요.
기사	네, 알겠습니다. 어디에 세워 드릴까요?
이준기	저기 보이는 흰 건물 앞에 세워 주세요. 얼마예요?
기사	만삼천 원입니다.
이준기	여기 있습니다. 감사합니다.
기사	감사합니다. 안녕히 가세요.

Write your own taxi conversation using the one on the previous page as a model.

가   _____ .

나   _____ .

가   _____ .

나   _____ .

가   _____ .

나   _____ .

연습해 보기 Let's Practice

Imagine that your friends are going somewhere by taxi. Fill in the chart with your ideas and then create a conversation. You can also make a short paragraph summarizing the conversation as in the example shown below.

질문 \ 친구	1) 스테파니	2)	3)
어디로 갈까요?	여의도		
어디에서 세워 드릴까요?	KBS 앞		

A

택시 기사	손님, 어디로 갈까요?
스테파니	여의도로 가 주세요.
택시 기사	손님, 어디에서 세워 드릴까요?
스테파니	KBS 앞에서 세워 주세요.

B

스테파니 씨는 여의도에 가고 싶어 해요.
KBS 앞에서 내릴 거예요.

Lee Joon-gi's Guide to Korea

Gyeongju

City of School Trips and Home of Bulguksa Temple

Mention Gyeongju, and most Koreans will think of school trips and Bulguksa Temple. This reflects the fact that the city is a hugely important tourist site and that Bulguksa Temple is a must-see on any visit there.

Early in Korean history, there were three countries on the Korean peninsula—Goguryeo, Baekje and Silla—which were eventually united by Silla. The capital of Silla from 57 BC to AD 935 was Gyeongju, and the culture of Silla flourished for a thousand years. A while back, I was watching a TV program that said that the culture of Silla was able to thrive because its people valued natural beauty and human dignity. Two of the best examples of this cultural brilliance are Bulguksa Temple and Cheomseongdae, the oldest astronomical observatory in Asia.

You know, I've been wondering something. Why is it that people get so excited about visiting famous historical sites such as those found in Greece? Is it the human desire to locate a beauty or a value that transcends time and space? Just as Europe has Greece, Asia has Gyeongju. Whenever you come here, you will be captured by its quiet charm.

Cheomseongdae is the oldest astronomical observatory in East Asia. ▶

함께 떠나요!

Bulguksa Temple is Gyeongju's most famous historical site.

Making a Phone Call
전화 걸기

거기 퍼디 씨
댁이지요 ?
Is This
Ferdy's
House?

Learning Objective
- - - - - - - - - - - - -
Situation
Making a phone call
Vocabulary
Leisure activities
Grammar
Possessive marker
Question tags
And/but

ONLINE
AUDIO
00:10

최지영 choejiyeong	여보세요. 거기 퍼디 씨 댁이지요? **yeoboseyo. geogi peodi ssi daegijiyo** *Hello. Is this Ferdy's house?*
어머니 eomeoni	네, 그렇습니다. 실례지만 누구세요? **ne, geureoseumnida. sillyejiman nuguseyo** *Yes that's right. May I ask who is calling?*
최지영 choejiyeong	저는 최지영입니다. 퍼디 씨의 친구예요. 퍼디 씨 계세요? **jeoneun choejiyeongimnida. peodi ssiui chinguyeyo. peodi ssi gyeseyo** *It's Jiyoung Choi. I'm Ferdy's friend. Is Ferdy there?*
어머니 eomeoni	아! 최지영 씨, 오랜만이에요. 잠시만 기다리세요. **a! choejiyeong ssi, oraenmanieyo. jamsiman gidariseyo** *Ah, Jiyoung. It's been a while. Just a moment.*
퍼디 peodi	최지영 씨 안녕하세요? 저예요. **choejiyeong ssi annyeonghaseyo? jeoyeyo** *Hi Jiyoung. It's me.*
최지영 choejiyeong	퍼디 씨, 지난 주말에 뭐 하셨어요? **peodi ssi, jinan jumare mwo hasyeosseoyo** *Ferdy what did you do last weekend?*
퍼디 peodi	친구들과 같이 <난타>를 봤는데 아주 재미있었어요. **chingudeulgwa gachi <nanta>reul bwanneunde aju jaemiisseosseoyo** *I went to see Nanta with my friends. It was a lot of fun.*
최지영 choejiyeong	어머! 저도 지난달에 봤는데 아주 재미있었어요. 그런데 퍼디 씨, 내일 동대문 시장에 가는데 같이 갈까요? **eomeo! jeodo jinandare bwanneunde aju jaemiisseosseoyo. geureonde peodi ssi, naeil dongdaemun sijange ganeunde gachi galkkayo** *Whoa. I saw that last month as well. It was a lot of fun. By the way Ferdy, tomorrow I'm going to Dongdaemun Market. Would you like to go together?*
퍼디 peodi	네, 좋아요. 같이 갑시다. 내일 다시 전화하겠습니다. **ne, joayo. gachi gapsida. naeil dasi jeonhwahagetseumnida** *Sure, that sounds great. Let's go together. I'll call you tomorrow.*

Vocabulary and Expressions 어휘와 표현

ONLINE AUDIO
02:38

01 명사 myeongsa — Nouns

집 〔집〕 **jip** *house*　　　　　　　　　　댁 〔댁〕 **daek** *house (honorific)*

*난타 〔난타〕 **nanta** *Nanta (a percussion show)*

동대문시장 〔동대문시장〕 **dongdaemun sijang** *Dongdaemun Market*

휴일 **hyuil** 〔휴일〕 *a day off*

시사회 〔시사회〕 **sisahoe** *a press screening of a movie*

닭갈비 〔닥깔비〕 **dakgalbi** *dalkgalbi (pan-fried chicken)*

초대장 〔초대짱〕 **chodaejang** *an invitation*　　이메일 **imeil** 〔이메일〕 *email*

남이섬 〔나미섬〕 **namiseom** *Nami Island (a tourist destination outside of Seoul)*

기차 〔기차〕 **gicha** *train*　　　　　　　배 〔배〕 **bae** *boat*

침대 〔침대〕 **chimdae** *bed*　　　　　단풍 〔담풍〕 **danpung** *autumn leaves*

*Nanta is a percussion-based show based on the traditional Korean music called samulnori. The show tells a humorous story that takes place in a kitchen. There is a Nanta performance hall in the Hongdae neighborhood of Seoul.

02 동사 dongsa — Verbs

배를 타다 〔배를타다〕 **baereul tada** *to get on a boat*

산책하다 〔산채카다〕 **sanchaekada** *to go for a walk*

농구를 하다 〔농구를하다〕 **nonggureul hada** *to play basketball*

즐겁다 〔즐겁따〕 **jeulgeopda** *to be enjoyable, to be fun*

뮤지컬을 보다 〔뮤지커를보다〕 **myujikeoreul boda** *to see a musical*

박물관에 가다 〔방물과네가다〕 **bangmulgwane gada** *to go to a museum*

기다리다 〔기다리다〕 **gidarida** *to wait*

눕다 〔눕따〕 **nupda** *to lie down*

초대장을 보내다 〔초대짱을보내다〕 **chodaejangeul bonaeda** *to send an invitation*

03 형용사 hyeongyongsa — Adjectives

지루하다 〔지루하다〕 **jiruhada** *to be boring*　　무섭다 〔무섭따〕 **museopda** *to be scary*

슬프다 〔슬프다〕 **seulpeuda** *to be sad*　　　쓸쓸하다 〔쓸쓸하다〕 **sseulsseulhada** *to be lonely*

괴롭다 〔괴롭따〕 **goeropda** *to be in pain, to be distressed*

힘들다 〔힘들다〕 **himdeulda** *to have a hard time*

괜찮다 〔괜찬타〕 **gwaenchanta** *to be OK, to be alright*

상쾌하다 〔상쾌하다〕 **sangkwaehada** *to be refreshing*

매력 있다 〔매려긷따〕 **maeryeok itda** *to be attractive*

매력 없다 〔매려겁따〕 **maeryeok eopda** *to be unattractive*

수업이 없다 〔수어비업따〕 **sueobi eopda** *there is no class (in school)*

04 기타 gita   **Miscellaneous**

여보세요 〔여보세요〕 **yeoboseyo** *Hello? (when answering the phone)*

실례지만 〔실례지만/실레지만〕 **sillyejiman** *Excuse me*

누구세요? 〔누구세요〕 **nuguseyo** *Who is this?*

계세요 〔계세요/게세요〕 **gyeseyo** *She/he is here*

안 계세요 〔앙계세요/앙게세요〕 **an gyeseyo** *She/he is not here*

오랜만이에요 〔오램마니에요〕 **oraenmanieyo** *It has been a long time*

잠시만 기다리세요 〔잠시만기다리세요〕 **jamsiman gidariseyo** *Just a moment*

다시 전화하겠습니다 〔다시전화하겓씀니다〕 **dasi jeonhwahagetseumnida** *I will call again*

발·음·규·칙 Pronunciation Rules

장애음의 비음화 Nasalization of obstruents
When the final consonant is ㅂ, ㄷ or ㄱ and the initial sound of the next syllable is ㅁ or ㄴ, the plosives ㅂ, ㄷ and ㄱ are pronounced as nasals ㅁ, ㄴ and ㅇ.

$$봤는데 \Rightarrow 〔받는데〕$$

$$ㄷ(ㅅ, ㅆ, ㅈ, ㅊ, ㅌ, ㅎ)+ㄴ \Rightarrow ㄴ+ㄴ$$

한국말 한ː궁말 **hangungmal** *Korean language*
믿는다 민는다 **minneunda** *I believe*
입는 임는 **imneun** *wearing*

Grammar 문법

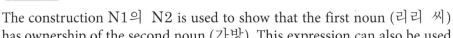

01 N의N NuiN   **Possessive marker**

리리 씨의 가방

Situation

The bag that is there belongs to Lili. You say: 리리 씨의 가방이에요. Lili's friend Stephanie is here." You say: 스테파니는 리리 씨의 친구예요.

Explanation

The construction N1의 N2 is used to show that the first noun (리리 씨) has ownership of the second noun (가방). This expression can also be used to indicate the social relationship, friendship or family ties between two individuals as we see in 리리 씨의 친구 스테파니 and 스테파니 씨의 친구 리리. The equivalent expression in English is 's and the order of the nouns is the same ("Lili's friend").

* Just a second! The pronouns 나의 and 저의 and 너의 can also be used in the shortened forms 내 and 제 and 네.

리리 씨의 친구

■ 소유 Possession

리리 씨의 가방이에요.
riri ssiui gabangieyo
It is Lili's bag.

제 커피예요.
je keopiyeyo
It is my coffee.

스테파니 씨의 구두예요.
seutepani ssiui guduyeyo
They are Stephanie's shoes.

■ 사회적인 관계 Social Relations

제 친구예요.
  je chinguyeyo
  (She/he) is my friend.

비비엔 씨의 선생님이에요.
  bibien ssiui seonsaengnimieyo
  (She/he) is Vivien's teacher.

퍼디 씨의 누나예요.
  peodi ssiui nunayeyo
  (She) is Ferdy's older sister.

02 N(이)지요? A/V-지요? N(i)jiyo? A/V-jiyo? Question tags

Situation

You're not sure if Lili is a student. You say: 리리 씨 학생이지요? You and your friend have heard that department stores are expensive in Korea, but you're not sure. You say: 백화점이 비싸지요?

Explanation

These two constructions are used when the speaker wants the listener to confirm that what they are saying is actually true. N(이)지요? is the form used with nouns, while A/V-지요? is used with verbs and adjectives. In English N(이)지요 A/V-지요 are rendered using question tags such as "isn't it?" "doesn't it?" and so forth.

리리 씨 학생이지요?

백화점이 비싸지요?

앙리 씨는 프랑스 사람이지요?
angni ssineun peurangseu saramijiyo
Henry is French, isn't he?

퍼디 씨는 의사지요?
peodi ssineun uisajiyo
Ferdy is a doctor, isn't he?

주말에 바다에 가지요?
jumare badae gajiyo
You are going to the seaside at the weekend, aren't you?

아침보다 기분이 좋지요?
achimboda gibuni jochiyo
You feel better than this morning, don't you?

■ How to make N(이)지요? N이었지요?/였지요?

In the present tense use N이지요? when there is a final consonant in the last syllable of the noun and N지요? when there is not. In the past tense use N이었지요? when there is a final consonant and N였지요? when there is not.

Final Consonant + 이지요?/이었지요?: 학생 → 학생이지요? 학생이었지요?

No Final Consonant + 지요?/였지요?: 의사 → 의사지요? 의사였지요?

■ How to make A/V-지요?, A/V-았/었지요?

For the present tense of adjectives and verbs, use A/V-지요? whether or not there is a final consonant. For the past tense, use A/V-았지요? when the vowel of the final syllable is a ㅏ or ㅗ, and use A/V-었지요? when it is not.

Final Consonant + 지요?: 덥다 → 덥다 + 지요? → 덥지요?

No Final Consonant + 지요?: 비싸다 → 비싸다 + 지요? → 비싸지요?

ㅏ, ㅗ일 때 + 았지요?: 보다 → 보다 + 았지요? → 봤지요?

ㅏ, ㅗ가 아닐 때 + 었지요?: 재미있다 → 재미있다 + 었지요? → 재미있었지요?

활용 연습 I Usage Practice 1

Fill in the blanks. Find the answers on page 255.

Base Form	N(이)지요?	N이었지요?/였지요?
의사	의사지요?	의사였지요?
친구		
선배		
학생		
선생님		

Base Form	A/V-지요?	A/V-았/었지요?
비싸다	비싸지요?	비쌌지요?
아프다		
많다		
괜찮다		
쓸쓸하다		
힘들다		
괴롭다		

03 N 인데, V- 는데, A-(으) ㄴ데   N inde, V-neunde, A-(eu)nde   And/but

Situation

Tomorrow is the weekend. You ask your friend to go with you to Gyeongbokgung Palace. You say:
내일은 주말인데 우리 같이 경복궁에 갈까요?
You went to see the percussion show *Nanta* yesterday. It was a lot of fun. You say:
어제 난타를 봤는데 아주 재미있었어요.

Explanation

The constructions N 인데, V– 는데 and A-(으) ㄴ데 are used to join groups of sentences like the ones in the examples above. Here, the first sentence serves as the premise for the explanation, suggestion, or command that comes in the second sentence. In short, the first sentence provides background for the second sentence. This is a nuance in Korean that is not explicitly expressed in English syntax.

내일은 주말인데 같이 난타를 볼까요?
naeireun jumarinde gachi nantareul bolkkayo
It's the weekend tomorrow, shall we go to see Nanta?

스테파니 씨의 친구인데 스테파니 씨 계세요?
seutepani ssiui chinguinde seutepani ssi gyeseyo
I am Stephanie's friend, is she here?

내일 명동에 가는데 같이 갑시다.
naeil myeongdonge ganeunde gachi gapsida
I am going to Myeongdong tomorrow, let's go together.

오늘 날씨가 추운데 다음 주에 만날까요?
oneul nalssiga chuunde daeum jue mannalkkayo
It's very cold today, shall we meet next week?

■ How to make N인데, N이었는데/였는데?

The present tense form N인데 is the same whether or not there is a final consonant in the last syllable of the noun. In the past tense, use N이었는데 when there is a final consonant and N였는데 when there is not.

Final Consonant + 인데/이었는데: 주말 → 주말인데, 주말이었는데

No Final Consonant + 인데/였는데: 친구 → 친구인데, 친구였는데

활용 연습 2 Usage Practice 2

Fill in the blanks. Find the answers on page 255.

Base Form	N인데	N이었는데/였는데
의사	의사인데	의사였는데
학교		
휴일		
주말		
시험		

■ How to make V-는데, V-았/었는데?

In the present tense, use V-는데 whether or not there is a final consonant in the last syllable of the verb. In the past tense of verbs, use V-았는데 when the vowel of the final syllable is ㅏ or ㅗ and V-었는데 when it is not.

Final Consonant + 는데: 먹다 → 먹다 + 는데 → 먹는데

No Final Consonant + 는데: 가다 → 가다 + 는데 → 가는데

Final Consonant + 르 → ㄹ + 는데: 만들다 → 만들다 + 는데 → 만드는데

ㅏ, ㅗ일 때 + 았는데: 자다 → 자다 + 았는데 → 잤는데

ㅏ, ㅗ가 아닐 때 + 었는데: 입다 → 입다 + 었는데 → 입었는데

하다 → 했는데 : 일하다 → 일하다 + 했는데 → 일했는데

Final Consonant + ㄷ → ㄹ + 었는데: 걷다 → 걷다 + ㄹ었는데 → 걸었는데

Final Consonant + ㅂ → 우 + 었는데: 눕다 → 눕다 + 웠 (우+었)는데 → 누웠는데

■ How to make A-(으)ㄴ데, A-았/었는데

Use A-은데 when there is a final consonant in the last syllable of the adjective stem and A-ㄴ데 when there is not. In the past tense form, use A-았는데 when the vowel of the final syllable is ㅏ or ㅗ and A-었는데 when it is not.

Final Consonant + 은데: 많다 → 많다 + 은데 → 많은데

No Final Consonant + ㄴ데: 비싸다 → 비싸다 + ㄴ데 → 비싼데

Final Consonant ㄹ → ㄹ + 는데: 멀다 → 멀다 + ㄴ데 → 먼데

Final Consonant ㅂ → 우 +: 춥다 → 춥다 + 운데 → 추운데

~있다 → ~있는데: 맛있다 → 맛있다 + 있는데 → 맛있는데

~없다 → ~없는데: 맛없다 → 맛없다 + 없는데 → 맛없는데

ㅏ, ㅗ일 때 + 았는데: 많다 → 많다 + 았는데 → 많았는데

ㅏ, ㅗ가 아닐 때 + 었는데: 멀다 → 멀다 + 었는데 → 멀었는데

하다 → 했는데: 따뜻하다 → 따뜻하다 + 했는데 → 따뜻했는데

Final Consonant ㅂ → 우 + 었는데: 맵다 → 맵다 + 웠 (우 + 었)는데 → 매웠는데

활용 연습 3 Usage Practice 3

Fill in the blanks. Find the answers on page 255.

Base Form	V-는데	V-았/었는데
뮤지컬을 보다	뮤지컬을 보는데	뮤지컬을 봤는데
친구를 기다리다		
커피를 마시다		
농구를 하다		
침대에 눕다		
꿈을 꾸다		

Base Form	A-(으)ㄴ데	A-았/었는데
기분이 좋다	기분이 좋은데	기분이 좋았는데
학교가 멀다		
날씨가 덥다		
영화가 재미있다		
돈이 없다		
조용하다		

Conversation Practice 회화 연습

01 리리 씨의 친구지요 ?   riri ssiui chingujiyo   **You're Lili's friend, aren't you?**

Use the example sentences to guide you as you practice. Find model sentences on page 255.

가: 리리 씨의 친구지요?
riri ssiui chingujiyo
You're Lili's friend, aren't you?

나: 네, 맞아요.
ne, majayo
Yes, I am.

가: 요즘 날씨가 춥지요?
yojeum nalssiga chupjiyo
It's cold these days, isn't it?

나: 아니요, 따뜻해요.
aniyo, ttatteuthaeyo
No, it's warm.

가: _____ ?

나: _____ .

가: _____ ?

나: _____ .

가: _____ ?

나: _____ .

가: _____?

나: _____.

커피를 마시다 x
차를 마시다 o

가: _____?

나: _____.

만들어 보세요.

예

일지매 팬이다 x
이준기 팬이다 o

차를 타다 x
걷다 o

요가를 하다 x
수영을 하다 o

잠을 자다 x
운동을 하다 o

록 음악을 듣다 x
한국 노래를 듣다 o

02 내일은 주말인데 바다에 갈까요? naeireun jumarinde badae galkkayo

It's the weekend tomorrow, shall we go to the beach?

Use the example sentences to guide you as you practice. Find model sentences on page 255.

내일, 주말 바다에 가다

가: 스테파니 씨, 내일은 주말인데 바다에 갈까요?
seutepani ssi, naeireun jumarinde badae galkkayo
Stephanie, it's the weekend tomorrow, shall we go to the beach?

나: 네, 좋아요. 바다에 갑시다.
ne, joayo. Badae gapsida
Yes, great. Let's go to the beach.

내일, 휴일 뮤지컬을 보다

가: 스테파니 씨, _____ ?

나: _____ .

오늘, 리리 씨의 생일 파티하다

가: _____ , _____ ?

나: _____ .

다음주, 시험 같이 공부하다

가: _____ , _____ ?

나: _____ .

만들어 보세요.
다음주
비비엔/생일
초대장을 보내다
…

가: _____ , _____ ?

나: _____ .

03   오늘 오후에 동대문 시장에 가는데 같이 갈까요?   I'm going to Dongdaemun Market this afternoon, shall we go together?
oneul ohue dongdaemun sijange ganeunde gachi galkkayo

Use the example sentences to guide you as you practice. Find model sentences on page 255.

가: 스테파니 씨, 오늘 오후에 동대문 시장에 가는데 같이 갈까요?
seutepani ssi, oneul ohue dongdaemun sijange ganeunde gachi galkkayo
Stephanie, I'm going to Dongdaemun Market this afternoon, shall we go together?

나: 네, 좋아요. 같이 갑시다.
ne, joayo. Gachi gapsida
Yes, great. Let's go together.

오늘 오후
동대문 시장에 가다
같이 가다

이번 주말
여의도에 가다
같이 가다

가: 스테파니 씨, _____

_____ ?

나: 네, 좋아요. _____ .

내일
박물관에 가다
같이 가다

가: _____ , _____

_____ ?

나: _____ .

오늘
바쁘다
내일 만나자

가: _____ , _____

_____ ?

나: _____ .

내일
수업이 없다
농구를 하다

가: _____ , _____

_____ ?

나: _____ .

만들어 보세요.
오늘
이준기를 만나다
같이 만나다
...

가: _____ , _____

_____ ?

나: _____ .

---

04 난타를 봤는데 재미있었어요 .
nantareul bwanneunde jaemiisseosseoyo

I went to see *Nanta* and it was fun.

Use the example sentences to guide you as you practice. Find model sentences on page 255.

지난 주말
난타를 보다
재미있다

가: 스테파니 씨, 지난 주말에 뭐 하셨어요?
seutepani ssi, jinan jumare mwo hasyeosseoyo
Stephanie, what did you do last weekend?

나: 저는 지난 주말에 난타를 봤는데 재미있었어요.
**jeoneun jinan jumare nantareul bwanneunde
jaemiisseosseoyo**
I went to see Nanta last weekend and it was fun.

지난 주말
롯데월드에 가다
아주 즐겁다

가: 리리 씨, _____ ?

나: _____ .

어제
영화를 보다
너무 슬프다

가: 하즈키 씨, _____ ?

나: _____ .

어제
불고기를 먹다
아주 맛있다

가: 요나단 씨, _____ ?

나: _____ .

가: _____ , _____

나: _____ .

만들어 보세요.

Listening Practice 듣기 연습

ONLINE AUDIO
05:26

Listen to the online audio file and answer the questions. You can find the audio script on page 241.

문제 1 두 사람은 지난 주말에 뭐 했어요?

1) 준이치: _____

2) 스테파니: _____

문제 2 두 사람은 내일 같이 뭐 해요?

_____

_____

Talking with Lee Joon-gi 이준기와 이야기하기

Try having a conversation with Lee Joon-gi as you listen to the audio. You can find a translation of this conversation on page 247.

스테파니　여보세요. 거기 이준기 씨 댁이지요?

어머니　네, 그렇습니다. 실례지만 누구세요?

스테파니　저는 스테파니입니다. 이준기 씨의 친구예요.
　　　　이준기 씨 계세요?

어머니　아! 스테파니 씨, 오랜만이에요. 잠시만 기다리세요.

이준기　스테파니 씨 안녕하세요? 저예요.

스테파니　준기 씨, 지난 주말에 뭐 하셨어요?

이준기　베이징에서 영화 촬영을 했는데 아주 힘들었어요.

스테파니　저는 친구들과 같이 바다에 갔는데 아주 아름다웠어요.

이준기　아, 그렇군요! 그런데 스테파니 씨 무슨 일이에요?

스테파니　준기 씨, 내일은 휴일인데 뭐 하실 거예요?

이준기　영화 시사회를 하는데 같이 갈까요?

스테파니　네, 좋아요. 같이 갑시다.

연습해 보기 Let's Practice

Read Stephanie's journal and then write a journal entry of your own.

저는 지난 주말에 비비엔이랑 벤슨하고 같이 남이섬에 갔어요.

우리는 기차와 버스, 그리고 배를 타고 남이섬에 갔어요.

우리는 남이섬에서 산책을 하고, 사진을 찍었는데 남이섬은 아주 아름다웠어요.

그리고 춘천닭갈비를 먹었는데 닭갈비는 맵지만 아주 맛있었어요.

아주 즐거운 여행이었어요. 다음에 또 가고 싶어요.

Lee Joon-gi's Guide to Korea

Incheon

An International City with Rock and K-Pop Festivals

Anyone who has visited Korea has heard of Incheon, since the city is the location of Incheon International Airport, the gateway to the country. When you reach Incheon Airport, you will probably feel nervous and excited if you're arriving, or laid-back and relaxed if you're coming home. When I leave Korea, I feel excited about the new things I'm about to do, and when I return to Korea, I feel satisfied to have finished another project and am ready to go home and relax for a while. I guess it might be just the opposite for non-Koreans, though!

Incheon has become a gathering place for young people, not only from Korea but from around the world. One reason for this is the prestigious Korean and foreign universities and international schools located in the new smart city of Songdo. Another reason is the Pentaport Rock Festival held each summer, which you might call the Woodstock of Korea, where you can feel an emotional connection as you sing along with the artists performing. With more K-Pop festivals being held in the area lately, I hope that it will become a place for young people from around the world to come together to share ideas and passions.

함께
떠나요!

Incheon Airport at night. The airport is the gateway to Korea.

There is a mysterious emotional connection between the musicians on stage and the young people in the crowd.

Seeing a Doctor
진찰받기

머리가 아프고
기침이 나요
**I Have a
Headache
and a Cough**

Learning Objective

Situation
Seeing a doctor
Vocabulary
Medical professionals
Hospitals
Diseases
Medication
Symptoms
Parts of the body
Grammar
Permission
Not allowed

✳✳✳ 병원에서 **byeongwoneseo** *At the Hospital* ✳✳✳

ONLINE
AUDIO
00:10

의사 uisa	어디가 아프세요? **eodiga apeuseyo?** *What seems to be the matter?*
요나단 yonadan	어제부터 목이 아프고 기침이 나요. **eojebuteo mogi apeugo gichimi nayo** *Since yesterday, I have a sore throat and a cough.*
의사 uisa	한 번 봅시다. 아! 목감기예요. **han beon bopsida. a! mokgamgiyeyo** *Let's take a look. Ah, your throat is sore because you have a cold.*
요나단 yonadan	오늘 저녁에 친구하고 약속이 있어요. 술을 마셔도 돼요? **oneul jeonyeoge chinguhago yaksogi isseoyo. sureul masyeodo dwaeyo** *This evening I have plans with a friend. Is it OK to drink alcohol?*
의사 uisa	술을 마시면 안 돼요. 담배도 피우면 안 돼요. **sureul masimyeon an dwaeyo. dambaedo piumyeon an dwaeyo** *You shouldn't drink. You shouldn't smoke, either.*
	이것은 처방전입니다. 약국에 가서 약을 받으세요. **igeoseun cheobangjeonimnida. yakguge gaseo yageul badeuseyo.** *Here is your prescription. Go to the pharmacy and get some medicine.*
요나단 yonadan	네, 알겠습니다. 감사합니다. **ne, algetseumnida. gamsahamnida** *Alright. Thank you.*

(continues overleaf)

✱ ✱ ✱ 약국에서 **yakgugeseo** *At the Pharmacy* ✱ ✱ ✱

약사
yaksa
처방전을 보여 주세요.
cheobangjeoneul boyeo juseyo
Let me see your prescription.

요나단
yonadan
여기 있어요.
yeogi isseoyo
Here it is.

약사
yaksa
요나단 씨, 감기약입니다.
yonadan ssi, gamgiyagimnida
Jonathan, here is your cold medicine.

요나단
yonadan
언제, 어떻게 먹어요?
eonje, eotteoke meogeoyo
When and how should I take it?

약사
yaksa
하루에 세 번 식후에 드세요.
harue se beon sikue deuseyo
Take it three times a day after meals.

요나단
yonadan
네, 감사합니다.
ne, gamsahamnida
Alright, thanks.

Vocabulary and Expressions 어휘와 표현

ONLINE AUDIO
02:40

01 의료진 uiryojin   Medical professionals

의사 〔의사〕 **uisa** *doctor*   주치의 〔주치의/주치이〕 **juchiui** *family physician*
약사 〔약싸〕 **yaksa** *pharmacist*   간호사 〔가노사〕 **ganhosa** *nurse*
*간병인 〔감병인〕 **ganbyeongin** *caregiver*   환자 〔환자〕 **hwanja** *patient*

02 병원의 종류 byeongwonui jongnyu   Hospital departments

내과 〔내:꽈〕 **naegwa** *internal medicine*   안과 〔앙:꽈〕 **angwa** *ophthalmology*
소아과 〔소:아꽈〕 **soagwa** *pediatrics*
외과 〔외:꽈/웨:꽈〕 **oegwa** *surgery*   치과 〔치꽈〕 **chigwa** *dentistry*
이비인후과 〔이:비인후꽈〕 **ibiinhugwa** *ENT (ear, nose and throat)*

03 병명 byeongmyeong   Names of diseases

감기 〔감기〕 **gamgi** *a cold*
목감기 〔목깜기〕 **mokgamgi** *sore throat (caused by a cold)*
코감기 〔코감기〕 **kogamgi** *runny nose (caused by a cold)*
몸살감기 〔몸살감기〕 **momsalgamgi** *aching all over (caused by a cold)*
눈병 〔눔뼝〕 **nunbyeong** *eye trouble*
소화불량 〔소화불량〕 **sohwabullyang** *indigestion*

04 약의 종류 yagui jongnyu   Kinds of medicine

알약 〔알략〕 **allyak** *pill*   가루약 〔가루약〕 **garuyak** *powdered medicine*
캡슐 〔캡쓜〕 **kaepsyul** *capsule*   물약 〔물략〕 **mullyak** *liquid medicine*
안약 〔아:냑〕 **anyak** *eye drops*   진통제 〔진통제〕 **jintongje** *painkiller*
소화제 〔소화제〕 **sohwaje** *digestive medicine* 파스 〔파스〕 **paseu** *pain-relief patch*
반창고 〔반창고〕 **banchanggo** *band-aid*   연고 〔영고〕 **yeongo** *ointment*
주사 〔주사〕 **jusa** *a shot, injection*   링거 〔링거〕 **ringgeo** *IV drip*

05 증상 **jeungsang**   **Symptoms**

머리가 아프다 〔머리가아프다〕
meoriga apeuda
to have a headache

이가 아프다 〔이가아프다〕
iga apeuda
to have a toothache

배가 아프다 〔배가아프다〕
baega apeuda
to have a stomachache

열이 나다 〔여리나다〕
yeori nada
to have a fever

기침이 나다 〔기치미나다〕
gichimi nada
to have a cough

메스껍다 〔메스껍따〕
meseukkeopda
to feel nauseous

토하다 〔토하다〕
tohada
to throw up

설사를 하다 〔설사를하다〕
seolsareul hada
to have diarrhea

식욕이 없다 〔시교기업따〕
singnyogi eopda
to have no appetite

콧물이 나다 〔콤무리나다〕
konmuri nada
to have a runny nose

코가 막히다 〔코가마키다〕
koga makida
a stuffy nose

어지럽다 〔어지럽따〕
eojireopda
to feel dizzy

감기에 걸리다 〔감기에걸리다〕
gamgie geollida
to catch a cold

오한이 나다 〔오하니나다〕
ohani nada
to have chills

목이 아프다 〔모기아프다〕
mogi apeuda
to have a sore throat

눈이 아프다 〔누니아프다〕
nuni apeuda
one's eyes hurt

눈물이 나다 〔눔무리나다〕
nunmuri nada
to have watery eyes

눈병에 걸리다 〔눔병에걸리다〕
nunbyeonge geollida
to get an eye infection

피가 나다 〔피가나다〕
piga nada
to bleed

다리가 아프다 〔다리가아프다〕
dariga apeuda
to have a sore leg

몸살이 나다 〔몸사리나다〕
momsari nada
to ache all over (from a fever)

---

06 기타 gita **Miscellaneous**

알약(가루약, 물약)을 먹다 〔알랴글먹따/가루랴글먹따/물랴글먹따〕
allyak (garuyak, mullyak)eul meokda
to take a pill (powdered medicine, capsule, liquid medicine)

안약을 넣다 〔아냐글너타〕 **anyageul neota** *to put in eye drops*

파스(반창고)를 붙이다 〔파스를부치다/반창고를부치다〕
paseu (banchanggo)reul buchida *to put on a pain-relief patch (band-aid)*

연고(물파스)를 바르다 〔영고를바르다/물파쓰를바르다〕
yeongo (mulpaseu)reul bareuda *to apply ointment (liquid for pain relief)*

처방전 〔처방전〕 **cheobangjeon** *prescription*   약국 〔약꾹〕 **yakguk** *pharmacy*

식전 〔식쩐〕 **sikjeon** *before eating*   식후 〔시쿠〕 **siku** *after eating*

돼지고기 〔돼지고기〕 **dwaejigogi** *pork*   전시실 〔전시실〕 **jeonsisil** *exhibition room*

휴게실 〔휴게실〕 **hyugesil** *rest area*   만지다 〔만지다〕 **manjida** *to touch*

07 신체 부위　sinche buwi　**Parts of the body**

머리 〔머리〕 **meori** *head*

코 〔코〕 **ko** *nose*

이 〔이〕 **i** *tooth*

목구멍 〔목꾸멍〕
　mokgumeong *throat*

등 〔등〕 **deung** *back*

팔꿈치 〔팔꿈치〕
　palkkumchi *elbow*

손바닥 〔솜빠닥〕
　sonbadak *palm*

손톱 〔손톱〕
　sontop *fingernail*

발목 〔발목〕 **balmok** *ankle*

발바닥 〔발빠닥〕 **balbadak**
　sole of the foot

발톱 〔발톱〕 **baltop** *toenail*

심장 〔심장〕 **simjang** *heart*

맹장 〔맹장〕 **maengjang**
　appendix

얼굴 〔얼굴〕 **eolgul** *face*

귀 〔귀〕 **gwi** *ear*

혀 〔혀〕 **hyeo** *tongue*

가슴 〔가슴〕 **gaseum** *chest*

어깨 〔어깨〕 **eokkae** *shoulder*

손목 〔솜목〕 **sonmok** *wrist*

손등 〔손뜽〕 **sondeung**
　back of the hand

다리 〔다리〕 **dari** *leg*

발꿈치 〔발꿈치〕 **balkkumchi** *heel*

발등 〔발뜽〕 **baldeung**
　instep

허리 〔허리〕 **heori**
　waist, lower back

폐 〔폐/페〕 **pye** *lungs*

눈 〔눈〕 **nun** *eye*

입 〔입〕 **ip** *mouth*

목 〔목〕 **mok** *neck*

배 〔배〕 **bae** *stomach*

팔 〔팔〕 **pal** *arm*

손 〔손〕 **son** *hand*

손가락 〔송까락〕
　songarak *finger*

무릎 〔무릅〕 **mureup** *knee*

발 〔발〕 **bal** *foot*

발가락 〔발까락〕
　balgarak *toe*

엉덩이 〔엉덩이〕
　eongdeongi *buttocks*

위장 〔위장〕 **wijang**
　stomach

발음규칙 **Pronunciation Rules**

격음화 **Aspiration**

When the consonants ㄱ, ㄷ, ㅂ or ㅈ appear immediately before or after ㅎ, they are pronounced together as ㅋ, ㅌ, ㅍ and ㅊ.

식후 ⇒ 〔시쿠

ㄱ + ㅎ ⇒ ㅋ

식후 시쿠 **siku** *after eating*
축하 추카 **chuka** *celebration*
백화점 배콰점 **baekwajeom** *department store*
특히 트키 **teuki** *especially*
좋고 조코 **joko** *good and*

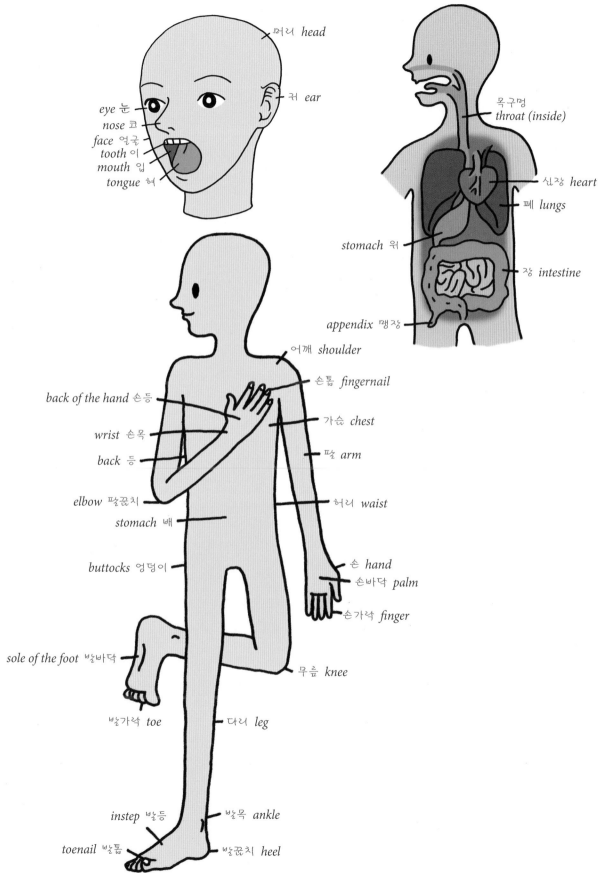

머리 head

귀 ear

eye 눈
nose 코
face 얼굴
tooth 이
mouth 입
tongue 혀

목구멍 throat (inside)

심장 heart

폐 lungs

stomach 위

장 intestine

appendix 맹장

어깨 shoulder

손톱 fingernail

back of the hand 손등

가슴 chest

wrist 손목

팔 arm

back 등

elbow 팔꿈치

허리 waist

stomach 배

buttocks 엉덩이

손 hand
손바닥 palm

손가락 finger

sole of the foot 발바닥

무릎 knee

발가락 toe

다리 leg

instep 발등

발목 ankle

toenail 발톱

발꿈치 heel

147

Chapter 08 **Seeing a Doctor**

Grammar 문법

01 V- 아 / 어도 되다 V-a/eodo doeda   Permission

Situation

You want to know if it's OK to drink coffee. You say: 커피를 마셔도 돼요? You want to tell someone else it's OK to drink. You say: 네, 마셔도 돼요.

Explanation

The V-아/어도 되다 construction is used when asking permission to do a certain action or giving someone else permission. In other words, this is how Koreans ask "Can I ____?" and answer "Yes, you can _____." (Don't confuse this with the other sense of "can," which means "able to," as in "birds can fly.")

커피를 마셔도 돼요?
keopireul masyeodo dwaeyo
Can I drink coffee?

사진을 찍어도 돼요.
sajineul jjigeodo dwaeyo
You can take a picture.

샤워해도 돼요.
syawohaedo dwaeyo
You can take a shower.

■ **How to make** V-아/어도 되다

Use V-아도 되다 when the vowel in the final syllable of the verb stem is ㅏ or ㅗ and use V-어도 되다 when it is not.

ㅏ, ㅗ일 때 + 아도 되다: 만나다 → 만나다 + 아도 되다 → 만나도 되다

ㅏ, ㅗ가 아닐 때+어도 되다: 먹다 → 먹다 + 어도 되다 → 먹어도 되다

~하다 → ~해도 되다: 운동하다 → 운동하다 + 해도 되다 → 운동해도 되다

Final Consonant is ㄷ → ㄹ + 어도 되다: 듣다 → 듣다 + ㄹ어도 되다 → 들어도 되다

Final Consonant ㅂ → 우 + 어도 되다: 줍다 → 줍다 + 워(우 + 어)도 되다 → 주워도 되다

148

활용 연습 I Usage Practice 1

Fill in the blanks. Find the answers on page 255.

Base Form	V-아/어도 돼요?	Base Form	V-아/어도 돼요?
커피를 마시다		만지다	
술을 마시다		복도에서 뛰다	
돼지고기를 먹다		샤워를 하다	
테니스를 치다	테니스를 쳐도 돼요?	떠들다	
담배를 피우다		앉다	
일하다		눕다	
수영하다		굽다	
사진을 찍다		걷다	
잠을 자다		닫다	

02 V-(으)면 안 되다 V-(eu)myeon an doeda **Not allowed**

Situation

As we learned in the last grammar point, when you are wondering if it's OK to take a picture you say, 사진을 찍어도 돼요? But if you want to tell someone it's not OK to do something, you say: 아니요, 사진을 찍으면 안 돼요.

Explanation

When someone has requested permission to do something or has asked whether a certain action is allowed, the construction V-(으)면 안 되다 is used to indicate that the action is prohibited.

사진을 찍으면 안 돼요.
sajineul jjigeumyeon an dwaeyo
You can't take a picture.

담배를 피우면 안 돼요.
dambaereul piumyeon an dwaeyo
You can't smoke.

술을 마시면 안 돼요?
sureul masimyeon an dwaeyo
Can't I drink?

■ How to make V-(으)면 안 되다

Use V-으면 안 되다 when there is a final consonant in the last syllable of the verb stem and use V-면 안 되다 when there is not.

Final Consonant 으면 안 되다: 먹다 → 먹다 + 으면 안 되다 → 먹으면 안 되다

No Final Consonant 면 안 되다: 보다 → 보다 + 면 안 되다 → 보면 안 되다

Final Consonant ㄹ + 면 안 되다: 만들다 → 만들다 + 면 안 되다 → 만들면 안 되다

Final Consonant ㄷ → ㄹ+ 으면 안 되다: 듣다 → 듣다 + ㄹ으면 안 되다 → 들으면 안 되다

Final Consonant ㅂ →우+면 안 되다: 줍다 → 줍다 + 우면 안 되다 → 주우면 안 되다

활용 연습 2 Usage Practice 2

Fill in the blanks. Find the answers on page 256.

Base Form	V-아/어도 돼요	Base Form	V-(으)면 안 돼요
커피를 마시다		만지다	
술을 마시다		복도에서 뛰다	복도에서 뛰면 안 돼요.
돼지고기를 먹다		샤워를 하다	
테니스를 치다		떠들다	
담배를 피우다		앉다	
일하다		눕다	
수영하다		굽다	
사진을 찍다		걷다	
잠을 자다		닫다	

Conversation Practice 회화 연습

01	머리가 아프고 기침이 나요.	I have a headache and a cough.
	meoriga apeugo gichimi nayo	

Use the example sentences to guide you as you practice. Find model sentences on page 256.

배가 아프다
식욕이 없다

가: 어디가 아프세요?
eodiga apeuseyo
What are your symptoms? [Lit. Where do you hurt?]

나: 저는 배가 아프고 식욕이 없어요.
jeoneun baega apeugo singnyogi eopseoyo
My stomach hurts and I have no appetite.

. . . .

머리가 아프다
열이 나다

가: 어디가 _____ ?

나: 저는 _____ .

. . . .

재채기가 나다
콧물이 나다

가: _____ ?

나: _____ .

. . . .

메스껍다
토하다

가: _____ ?

나: _____ .

. . . .

배가 아프다
설사를 하다

가: _____ ?

나: _____ .

. . . .

기침이 나다
오한이 나다

가: _____?

나: _____.

눈물이 나다
눈이 아프다

가: _____?

나: _____.

이가 아프다
피가 나다

가: _____?

나: _____.

만들어 보세요.

가: _____?

나: _____.

 예

어깨가
아프다

팔이 아프다

메스껍다

코가 막히다

기침이
나다

머리가
아프다

다리가
아프다

02 커피를 마셔도 돼요 ? **keopireul masyeodo dwaeyo** **Can I drink coffee?**

Use the example sentences to guide you as you practice. Find model sentences on page 256.

커피를 마시다 O

리리 씨, 커피를 마셔도 돼요?
riri ssi, keopireul masyeodo dwaeyo
Lili, can I have a coffee?

네, 커피를 마셔도 돼요.
ne, keopireul masyeodo dwaeyo
Yes, you can.

담배를 피우다 O

가: 리리 씨, _____?

나: 아니요, _____.

아이스크림을 먹다 O

가: _____ , _____?

나: _____.

샤워하다 O

가: _____ , _____?

나: _____.

술을 마시다 O

가: _____ , _____?

나: _____.

수영하다 ○

가: _____ , _____ ?

나: _____ .

가: _____ ?

나: _____ .

만들어 보세요.

자다 ○   예

쉬다 ○

사진을 찍다 ○

청소를 하다 ○

03 사진을 찍으면 안 돼요 .   sajineul jjigeumyeon an dwaeyo   **Can I take a picture?**

Use the example sentences to guide you as you practice. Find model sentences on page 256.

앙리 씨, 사진을 찍어도 돼요?
angni ssi, sajineul jjigeodo dwaeyo
Henry, can I take a picture?

아니요, 사진을 찍으면 안 돼요.
aniyo, sajineul jjigeumyeon an dwaeyo
No, you can't take a picture.

가: 앙리 씨, _____ ?

나: 아니요 _____ .

가: _____ , _____ ?

나: _____ .

가: _____ , _____ ?

나: _____ .

가: _____ , _____ ?

나: _____ .

숲을 마시다 ✗

가: _____ , _____ ?

나: _____ .

만들어 보세요.

가: _____ ?

나: _____ .

수영을 하다 ✗

예

산책을 하다 ✗

드럼을 치다 ✗

음악을 듣다 ✗

영화를 보다 ✗

Listening Practice 1 듣기 연습 1

ONLINE AUDIO
07:55

Listen to the online audio file and decide what is wrong with each person. Write the numbers of the ailments in the brackets. You can find the audio script on page 241.

문제 이 사람들은 어디가 아파요? 그림에서 번호를 골라 보기와 같이 써 보세요.

의사   어디가 아프세요?

스테파니   저는 머리가 아프고 열이 나요.

<보테기>   (①, ⑥) 스테파니 씨는 머리가 아프고 열이 나요.

1) 최지영: (,   ) _____고 _____.

2) 요나단: (,   ) _____고 _____.

3) 비비엔: (,   ) _____고 _____.

4) 벤 슨: (,   ) _____고 _____.

Listening Practice 2 듣기 연습 2

ONLINE AUDIO
09:34

Listen to the online audio file and write the answers to each question, referring to the numbered illustrations. You can find the audio script on page 241.

문제 1 전시실에서 할 수 없는 것은 무엇이에요? 그림을 보고 모두 고르세요.

문제 2 휴게실에서 할 수 있는 것은 무엇이에요? 그림을 보고 모두 고르세요.

Talking with Lee Joon-gi   이준기와 이야기하기

ONLINE AUDIO
11:19

Try having a conversation with Lee Joon-gi as you listen to the audio. You can find a translation of this conversation on page 247.

✳✳✳ 병원에서 ✳✳✳

의사	어디가 아프세요?
이준기	어제부터 눈이 아프고 눈물이 나요.
의사	한번 봅시다. 아! 요즘 유행하는 눈병이에요
이준기	오늘 오후에 영화 촬영이 있어요. 촬영장에 가도 돼요?
의사	밖에 나가면 안 돼요. 3일 정도 집에서 푹 쉬세요. 이것은 처방전입니다. 약국에 가서 약을 받으세요.
이준기	네, 알겠습니다. 감사합니다.

✳✳✳ 약국에서 ✳✳✳

의사	이준기 씨, 안약입니다. 두 시간에 한 번 눈에 넣으세요.
이준기	네, 감사합니다.

연습해 보기 1 Let's Practice 1

Roleplay doctor and patient, using the prompts in the boxes below. You can add your own questions in the parts that have a question mark. You can speak both parts aloud yourself, write the dialogues, or practice with a fellow student.

팀 의사	환자
1 병명: 감기 처방전: 감기약, 하루 3번 식후	언제부터: 어제 증상: 머리가 아프다/열이 나다 질문: 저녁에 회식이 있다 (술을 마시다, ?)
2 병명: 유행성 눈병 처방전: 안약, 1시간 1번씩	언제부터: 아침 증상: 눈이 아프다/눈물이 나다 질문: 내일 여행을 가다 (운전하다, ?)
3 병명: 소화불량 처방전: 소화제, 하루 3번 식전	언제부터: 지난 주말 증상: 식욕이 없다/토하다 질문: 저녁에 회식이 있다 (돼지고기를 먹다, ?)
4 병명: 두통 처방전: 진통제, 하루 3번 식후	언제부터: 2시간 전 증상: 머리가 아프다/어지럽다 질문: 오후에 외출하다 (수영하다, ?)

연습해 보기 2 Let's Practice 2

The table below gives information about the symptoms of illness and questions you want to ask the doctor. Create conversations following the example shown below.

의사	어디가 아프세요?
환자	열이 나고 머리가 아파요. 선생님, 샤워해도 돼요?
의사	네, 샤워해도 돼요.
환자	그럼, 술을 마셔도 돼요?
의사	아니요, 술을 마시면 안 돼요.

질문 \ 증상	열이 나다 머리가 아프다	토하다 배가 아프다	눈이 아프다 눈물이 나다
1) 술을 마시다	×		
2) 샤워하다	○		
3) 돼지고기를 먹다		○	
4) 수영하다			×
5) 담배를 피우다			
6) 아이스크림을 먹다		×	
7) 커피를 마시다			○

Busan

The City Where the Movie Stars of Asia Gather

Night and day in Busan are as different as, well, night and day. Take Busan's popular tourist spot, Jagalchi Fish Market, for example. During the daytime, visitors to the market can see the vigorous activity of Gyeongsang Province's *ajimae*, the term in the local dialect for middle-aged women. While they may be a bit rough around the edges, they are warm and friendly.

At night, visitors can head for Gwangalli Beach, and walk along the sand while admiring the nightscape of a city that dazzles with intrigue and beauty. Indeed, Busan is a place where urban architecture, seaside fish markets, and rustic views can be found all in one place. Perhaps it is this diversity that gives the city such delightful down-home dishes as pork and rice soup, seed hotteok, and fishcake.

But there's something else about Busan that makes the city even more thrilling for an actor like me. I'm talking about the Busan International Film Festival, which kicks off on the first Thursday of each October. During the festival, the city transforms into a galaxy of shining stars—movie stars, that is! Nothing beats the pleasure of rubbing shoulders with actors from Korea and abroad.

It's hard to describe how it feels to watch actors walking the red carpet—and to see major figures in the world of cinema and everyone else who loves n watching me walking that very same red carpet!

함께 떠나요!

Each year during the Busan Film Festival, the city of Busan is completely transformed.

At Jagalchi Market, you can feel the warmth of Gyeongsang Province's *ajimae* (middle-aged women).

Declining a Request
거절하기

미안하지만,
못 가요
I'm Sorry,
but I Can't Go

Learning Objective

Situation
Declining a request
Vocabulary
Sports
Excuses and reasons
Places
Grammar
Stating a purpose
Because

ONLINE
AUDIO
00:10

벤슨 benseun	아마니 씨, 무슨 운동을 좋아하세요? **amani ssi, museun undongeul joahaseyo** *Amani, what kind of sports do you like?*
아마니 amani	저는 골프를 좋아해요. **jeoneun golpeureul joahaeyo** *I like golf.*
벤슨 benseun	우아! 저도 골프를 좋아해요. 아마니 씨, 골프를 잘 치세요? **ua! jeodo golpeureul joahaeyo. amani ssi, golpeureul jal chiseyo** *Wow! I like golf, too. Amani, are you good at golf?*
아마니 amani	조금 쳐요. **jogeum chyeoyo** *I'm not bad.*
벤슨 benseun	그럼, 오늘 오후에 같이 골프를 치러 갈까요? **geureom, oneul ohue gachi golpeureul chireo galkkayo** *Well, would you like to go with me to play golf this afternoon?*
아마니 amani	미안하지만, 못 가요. **mianhajiman, mot gayo** *I'm sorry, but I can't go.*
벤슨 benseun	왜 못 가요? **wae mot gayo** *Why not?*
아마니 amani	약속이 있어서 못 가요. **yaksogi isseoseo mot gayo** *I can't go because I have other plans.*
벤슨 benseun	그럼, 다음 주말에 같이 갑시다. **geureom, daeum jumare gachi gapsida** *In that case, let's go together next weekend.*
아마니 amani	네, 좋아요. **ne, joayo** *That sounds great.*

Vocabulary and Expressions 어휘와 표현

ONLINE AUDIO
01:52

01 운동 undong Sports

보드 [보드] **bodeu** *snowboard*
눈썰매 [눈:썰매] **nunsseolmae** *sled*
스케이트 [스케이트] **seukeiteu** *skating, skates*
검도 [검도] **geomdo** *kendo*
요가 [요가] **yoga** *yoga*
볼링 [볼링] **bolling** *bowling*

02 동사 (운동) dongsa (undong) Verbs (Sports)

골프(테니스, 볼링)을/를 치다 [골프를치다/테니스를치다/볼링을치다]
  golpeu (teniseu, bolling)eul/reul chida
  to play golf (play tennis, go bowling)

스키(보드, 눈썰매, 스케이트)을/를 타다
  [스키를타다/보드를타다/눈:썰매를타다/스케이트를타다]
  seuki (bodeu, nunsseolmae, seukeiteu)eul/reul tada
  to go skiing (snowboarding, sledding, skating)

농구[태권도, 검도]을/를 하다 [농구를하다/태권도를하다/검도를하다]
  nonggu (taegwondo, geomdo)eul/reul hada
  to play basketball (practice taekwondo, practice kendo)

03 핑계 pinggye Excuses

숙제가 많다 [숙쩨가만타] **sukjega manta** *to have a lot of homework*
약속이 있다 [약쏘기읻따] **yaksogi itda** *to already have plans*
늦잠을 자다 [는짜믈자다] **neutjameul jada** *to sleep in*
알러지가 있다 [알러지가읻따] **alleojiga itda** *to have an allergy*
무섭다 [무섭따] **museopda** *to be afraid*
바쁘다 [바쁘다] **bappeuda** *to be busy*

04 이유 iyu Reasons

건강에 좋다 [겅강에조타] **geongange jota** *to be good for one, to be healthy*
다이어트에 좋다 [다이어트에조타] **daieoteue jota** *to help with one's diet*
피곤하다 [피곤하다] **pigonhada** *to be tired*

길이 막히다 〔기리마키다〕 **giri makida** *to have bad traffic*
먹기가 편하다 〔먹끼가편하다〕 **meokgiga pyeonhada** *to be easy to eat*

05 장소 jangso   Places

스키장 〔스키장〕 **seukijang** *skating rink*
체육관 〔체육꽌〕 **cheyukgwan** *gymnasium*
눈썰매장 〔눈:썰매장〕 **nunsseolmaejang** *a slope for sledding*
평창 〔평창〕 **pyeongchang** *Pyeongchang*

06 기타 gita   Miscellaneous

같이 〔가치〕 **gachi** *together, with someone*
미안하다 〔미안하다〕 **mianhada** *to be sorry*
왜 〔왜〕 **wae** *why*
생선회 〔생선회〕 **saengseonhoe** *sashimi*
글쎄요 〔글쎄요〕 **geulsseyo** *I'm not sure (used to avoid answering a question)*
계획 〔계획/게획〕 **gyehoek** *a plan*
조금 〔조금〕 **jogeum** *a little*
잘 〔잘〕 **jal** *well (as in "to do something well")*
연극을 보다 〔영그글보다〕 **yeongeugeul boda** *to watch a play*

발음규칙 Pronunciation Rules

구개음화 Palatalization
When final consonant ㄷ or ㅌ is followed by ㅇ it is pronounced as ㅈ, and when followed by ㅎ, it is pronounced as ㅊ.

$$같이 ⇒ 〔가치〕$$
$$ㅌ+이 ⇒ 치$$

같이 가치 **gachi** *together*
해돋이 해도지 **kkeuchi** *the end is*
해돋이 해도지 **haedoji** *sunrise*
굳히다 구치다 **guchida** *to harden*

Grammar 문법

01 V-(으)러 가다 / 오다 V-(eu)reo gada/oda Stating a purpose

Situation

You're going to the beach tomorrow so that you can go swimming and you're excited. You say: 저는 수영하러 바다에 가요. You're going to the library and looking forward to getting some good books to read. You say: 저는 책을 읽으러 도서관에 가요.

Explanation

The construction V-(으)러 comes before a verb of motion such as 가다, 오다, 다니다, 나가다, 나오다, 들어가다 or 들어오다 and tells what the purpose of that motion is. That is to say, the subject of the sentence performs the action in the second half of the sentence in order to accomplish the objective expressed in the first half of the sentence. In English, the infinitive form of the verb ("to V") is typically used, though "in order to V" is also possible.

리리 씨는 연극을 보러 대학로에 가요.
riri ssineun yeongeugeul boreo daehangnoe gayo
Lili is going to Daehangno to see a play.

저는 책을 사러 서점에 가요.
jeoneun chaegeul sareo seojeome gayo
I am going to the bookstore to buy a book.

스테파니 씨는 친구를 만나러 이태원에 가요.
seutepani ssineun chingureul mannareo itaewone gayo
Stephanie is going to Itaewon to meet her friend.

하즈키 씨는 공연을 보러 홍대에 가요.
hajeuki ssineun gongyeoneul boreo hongdaee gayo
Hazuki is going to Hongdae to see a performance.

■ How to make V-(으)러

V–으러 is used when there is a final consonant in the last syllable of the verb stem, while V–러 is used when there is no final consonant or when the final consonant is ㄹ.

Final Consonant + 으러: 먹다 → 먹다 + 으러 → 먹으러

No Final Consonant + 러: 보다 → 보다 + 러 → 보러

Final Consonant ㄹ + 러: 만들다 → 만들다 + 러 → 만들러

Final Consonant ㅂ → 우 + 러: 줍다 → 줍다 + 우러 → 주우러

Final Consonant ㄷ → ㄹ + 으러: 듣다 → 듣다 + ㄹ으러 → 들으러

활용 연습 1 Usage Practice 1

Fill in the blanks. Find the answers on page 256.

Base Form	V-(으)러 가요	Base Form	V-(으)러 가요
스키를 타다	스키를 타러 가요.	음악을 듣다	
번지점프를 하다		맥주를 마시다	
삼계탕을 먹다		친구를 돕다	
수영하다		태권도를 배우다	
김치를 담그다		책을 읽다	
옷을 사다		공연을 보다	
잠을 자다		쇼핑하다	

02 A/V- 아 / 어서   A/V-a/eoseo

Because

Situation

You have a lot of homework today so you can't play football.
You say: 오늘은 숙제가 많아서 축구를 못 해요.
You like pizza because it's delicious. You say: 맛있어서
피자를 좋아해요.

Explanation

The construction A/V-아/어서 generally expresses a reason
or excuse for what is said in the following clause. In the pre-
ceding examples, the reasons we see are 숙제가 많다 and 맛있다. In English, we use the coor-
dinating conjunction "so" if the reason comes first or the subordinating conjunction "because"
if the reason comes second.

오늘은 숙제가 많아서 못 가요.
oneureun sukjega manaseo mot gayo
I can't come today because I have a lot of homework.

매워서 못 먹어요.
maewoseo mot meogeoyo
I can't eat it because it is spicy.

따뜻해서 봄을 좋아해요.
ttatteuthaeseo bomeul joahaeyo
I like spring because it is warm.

■ How to make A/V-아/어서

Use V-아서 when the vowel in the last syllable of the verb or adjective stem is ㅏ or ㅗ, and
use V-어서 when it is not.

ㅏ, ㅗ일 때 + 아서: 만나다 → 만나다 + 아서 → 만나서

ㅏ, ㅗ가 아닐 때 + 어서: 먹다 → 먹다 + 어서 → 먹어서

~하다 → ~해서: 따뜻하다 → 따뜻하다 + 해서 → 따뜻해서

Final Consonant ㄷ → ㄹ + 어서: 묻다 → 묻다 + ㄹ어서 → 물어서

Final Consonant ㅂ → 우 + 어서: 덥다 → 덥다 + 워 (우+어)서 → 더워서

활용 연습 2 Usage Practice 2

Fill in the blanks. Find the answers on page 257.

Base Form	A/V-아/어서
손님이 오다	손님이 와서
감기에 걸리다	
늦잠을 자다	
길이 막히다	
맵다	
짧다	
줍다	
길다	
걷다	
조용하다	

Conversation Practice 회화 연습

01	감기에 걸려서 못 왔어요 . gamgie geollyeoseo mot wasseoyo	I couldn't come because I had a cold.

Use the example sentences to guide you as you practice. Find model sentences on page 257.

어제 학교에 안 오다
감기에 걸리다

가: 리리 씨, 어제 왜 학교에 안 왔어요?
riri ssi, eoje wae hakgyoe an wasseoyo
Lili, why didn't you come to school yesterday?

나: 저는 어제 감기에 걸려서 못 왔어요.
jeoneun eoje gamgie geollyeoseo mot wasseoyo
I couldn't come because I had a cold.

어제 축구를 안 하다
다리가 아프다

가: 준이치 씨, _____?

나: _____ .

오늘 영화를 안 보다
숙제가 많다

가: 앙리 씨, _____?

나: _____ .

주말에 롯데월드에 안 가다
바쁘다

가: 이준기 씨 _____?

나: _____ .

어제 수영을 안 하다
감기에 걸리다

가: 벤슨 씨, _____?

나: _____ .

오늘 밥을 안 먹다
배가 아프다

가: 리리 씨, _____?

나: _____.

만들어 보세요.

가: _____?

나: _____.

아침에 안 오다
늦잠을 자다

예

이준기
오늘 촬영을 안 하다
몸이 아프다

오늘 숙제를 안 하다
친구들과 늦게까지
놀다

아까 안 기다리다
수업이 있다

어제 약속시간에 안 오다
길이 너무 막히다

02 쇼핑하러 행복마트에 가요 .
syopinghareo haengbongmateue gayo

I'm going to Haengbok Market to do the shopping

Use the example sentences to guide you as you practice. Find model sentences on page 257.

가: 하즈키 씨, 어디에 가세요?
hajeuki ssi, eodie gaseyo
Hazuki, where are you going?

나: 저는 쇼핑하러 행복마트에 가요.
jeoneun syopinghareo haengbongmateue gayo
I am going to Haengbok Market to do the shopping.

가: 하즈키 씨, _____?

나: 저는 _____.

가: _____ , _____?

나: _____.

가: _____ , _____?

나: _____.

가: _____ , _____?

나: _____.

태권도를 하다
태권도장에 가다

가: _____ , _____?

나: _____ .

만들어 보세요.

가: _____?

나: _____ .

친구를 만나다
학교에 가다

콘서트 보다
콘서트장에 가다

(예)

공부하다
도서관에 가다

도서관

쇼핑하다
동대문 시장에 가다

Listening Practice 듣기 연습

ONLINE AUDIO
04:39

Listen to the online auiod files and write the answers to the questions. You can find the audio script on page 242.

문제 1 두 사람은 무슨 운동을 좋아해요?

문제 2 두 사람은 왜 이번 주에 같이 수영하러 안 가요?

문제 3 두 사람은 언제 같이 수영하러 가요?

Talking with Lee Joon-gi 1   이준기와 이야기하기 1

ONLINE AUDIO
06:49

Try having a conversation with Lee Joon-gi as you listen to the audio. You can find a translation of this conversation on page 247.

이준기	리리 씨, 이번 주말에 뭐 할 거예요?
리리	글쎄요! 아직 계획이 없어요. 이준기 씨는요?
이준기	저는 스키를 타러 평창에 갈 거예요.
리리	우아! 이준기 씨 스키를 잘 타세요?
이준기	그냥, 조금 타요. 리리 씨도 스키를 좋아하세요?
리리	네, 저도 스키를 좋아해요.
이준기	그럼, 리리 씨도 이번 주말에 같이 갈까요?
리리	미안하지만, 이번 주말에는 못 가요.
이준기	왜요?
리리	다리가 아파서 스키를 못 타요.
이준기	그럼, 다음 주말에 같이 갑시다.
리리	네, 좋아요.

Talking with Lee Joon-gi 2 이준기와 이야기하기 2

ONLINE AUDIO
08:20

Listen to Lee Joon-gi (on this page) and Vivien (opposite). Try having a conversation with Lee Joon-gi as you listen to the audio. Find translations of these conversation on pages 247–248.

이준기 제 이름은 이준기예요. 저는 한국 사람이에요.

요즘 영화 촬영을 하고 있어요.

저는 불고기를 아주 좋아해요.

불고기는 비싸지만 맛있어서 좋아해요.

저는 따뜻해서 봄을 좋아하고, 맛있어서 사과를 좋아해요.

그리고 건강에 좋아서 태권도를 아주 좋아해요.

하지만 요즘 바빠서 자주 못 해요.

이번 주말에는 태권도를 하러 태권도장에 갈 거예요.

그리고 친구를 만나러 부산에 갈 거예요.

부산에서 친구하고 같이 생선회를 먹을 거예요.

Talking with Lee Joon-gi 3   이준기와 이야기하기 3

ONLINE AUDIO
09:10

비비엔   제 이름은 비비엔이에요. 저는 독일 사람이에요.
한국대학교에서 한국어를 공부하고, DK스키장에서 스키를 가르쳐요.
저는 비빔밥을 아주 좋아해요.
비빔밥은 맵지만 야채가 많아서 좋아해요.
저는 눈이 와서 겨울을 좋아해요.
먹기가 편해서 바나나를 좋아해요.
그리고 다이어트에 좋아서 수영을 아주 좋아해요.
하지만 요즘 바빠서 자주 못 해요.
이번 주말에는 수영하러 수영장에 갈 거예요.
그리고 친구를 만나러 명동에 갈 거예요.
명동에서 친구하고 같이 무서운 영화를 볼 거예요.

연습해 보기 Let's Practice

Use the example sentences to guide you as you practice. It's even more helpful to do this with a friend who is studying Korean.

최지영   스테파니 씨, 무슨 운동을 좋아하세요?

스테파니 저는 야구를 좋아해요.

최지영   왜 야구를 좋아하세요?

스테파니 저는 재미있어서 야구를 좋아해요.

질문 \ 친구	1) 스테파니	2)	3)
1) 무슨 운동	야구/재미있다		
2) 무슨 과일	바나나/맛있다		
3) 무슨 음식	김밥/맛있다		
4) 무슨 계절	가을/단풍이 예쁘다		
5) 누구	이준기/잘생기다		

 Introduce your friends just as Jiyoung does.

최지영   스테파니 씨는 재미있어서 야구를 좋아해요.
         그리고 맛있어서 바나나와 김밥을 좋아하고,
         단풍이 예뻐서 가을을 좋아해요.
         그리고 잘생겨서 이준기를 좋아해요.

Andong Hahoe Village

Home of the Pungsan Ryu Clan for Generations

In Korea, villages that are filled with people with the same last name are referred to as *jipseong-chon*. Andong Hahoe Village is one good example, as it is where members of the Pungsan Ryu clan have lived for generations. Long ago in Korea, it was customary for relatives with the same family name to live together in one village. These days, people often move to new cities for work and for study, making it hard for families to maintain this tradition of living in the same place. This should give you an idea of how unique and precious Andong Hahoe Village is.

As you gaze at the houses built in the traditional style, some of straw and some of tile, you will find yourself drawn into the past. Peek through an open door into the courtyard of one of these old houses, and you might see the residents performing the Hahoe Mask Dance, wearing the traditional Hahoe mask, which is designed to look like a laughing human face. Watching this delightful dance is a great way to forget about your everyday problems.

The village has also gotten attention because of the visit of Queen Elizabeth II in 1999 and the fact that it is the ancestral home of Hallyu actor Ryu Si-won.

The people in the house are performing the Hahoe Mask Dance.

Describing What Someone Is Wearing
옷차림 말하기

Learning Objective

Situation
Describing clothes
Vocabulary
Colors
Clothes
Accessories
Verbs for clothing
Grammar
Am/are/is wearing
Who/which/that

ONLINE
AUDIO
00:10

이준기 ijungi	비비엔 씨, 이 사진은 뭐예요?
	bibien ssi, i sajineun mwoyeyo
	Vivien, what is this picture?

비비엔
bibien

이 사람들은 모두 제 친구들이에요. 지난주에 스테파니 씨의 생일 파티에서 찍은 사진이에요.

i saramdeureun modu je chingudeurieyo. jinanjue seutepani ssiui saengil patieseo jjigeun sajinieyo

These people are all my friends. It's a photo from Stephanie's birthday party last week.

이준기
ijungi

우아! 여기 파란 티셔츠를 입고 꽃무늬 넥타이를 매고 있는 사람은 누구예요?

ua! yeogi paran tisyeocheureul ipgo kkonmunui nektaireul maego inneun sarameun nuguyeyo

Wow! Who is the person here in a blue t-shirt and a flower-print tie?

비비엔
bibien

아! 그 사람은 앙리 씨예요.

a! geu sarameun angni ssiyeyo

Oh, that's Henri.

이준기
ijungi

아, 그렇군요! 그런데 스테파니 씨는 어디에 있어요?

a, geureokunyo! geureonde seutepani ssineun eodie isseoyo

Oh, I see! And where is Stephanie?

비비엔
bibien

여기 노란 원피스를 입고 있는 사람이에요.

yeogi noran wonpiseureul ipgo inneun saramieyo

She is the person here in the yellow dress.

이준기
ijungi

와! 스테파니 씨에게 노란색이 잘 어울리는군요!

wa! seutepani ssiege noransaegi jal eoullineungunyo

Aha! Yellow looks great on her.

비비엔
bibien

네, 아주 예쁘지요!

ne, aju yeppeujiyo

Yes, it's really pretty, isn't it?

Vocabulary and Expressions 어휘와 표현

ONLINE AUDIO
02:10

01 형용사 (색깔) hyeongyongsa (saekkkal) — Adjectives (Colors)

파랗다 〔파라타〕 **parata** *blue*　　노랗다 〔노라타〕 **norata** *yellow*

빨갛다 〔빨가타〕 **ppalgata** *red*　　하얗다 〔히야타〕 **hayata** *white*

까맣다 〔까마타〕 **kkamata** *black*　　새빨갛다 〔새빨가타〕 **saeppalgata** *bright red*

02 옷 ot — Clothing

넥타이 〔넥타이〕 **nektai** *necktie*　　스카프 〔스카프〕 **seukapeu** *scarf*

목도리 〔목또리〕 **mokdori** *muffler*　　양복 〔양복〕 **yangbok** *suit (for men)*

정장 〔정장〕 **jeongjang** *suit*　　원피스 〔웜피스〕 **wonpiseu** *dress*

티셔츠 〔티셔츠〕 **tisyeocheu** *T-shirt*　　와이셔츠 〔와이셔츠〕 **waisyeocheu** *dress shirt*

블라우스 〔브라우스〕 **beullauseu** *blouse*　　스웨터 〔스웨터〕 **seuweteo** *sweater*

치마 〔치마〕 **chima** *skirt*　　바지 〔바지〕 **baji** *pants*

양말 〔양말〕 **yangmal** *socks*　　스타킹 〔스타킹〕 **seutaking** *stockings*

레깅스 〔레깅스〕 **regingseu** *leggings*　　청바지 〔청바지〕 **cheongbaji** *jeans*

재킷 〔자켇〕 **jaket** *suit jacket, blazer*　　코트 〔코트〕 **koteu** *coat*

모자 〔모자〕 **moja** *hat*　　장갑 〔장갑〕 **janggap** *gloves*

상의 〔상이〕 **sangui** *top*　　하의 〔하이〕 **haui** *bottoms, pants*

03 액세서리류 aekseseoriryu — Accessories

목걸이 〔목꺼리〕 **mokgeori** *necklace*　　귀걸이 〔귀거리〕 **gwigeori** *earrings*

반지 〔반지〕 **banji** *ring*　　팔찌 〔팔찌〕 **paljji** *bracelet*

발찌 〔발찌〕 **baljji** *anklet*　　머리핀 〔머리핀〕 **meoripin** *hairpin*

머리띠 〔머리띠〕 **meoritti** *headband*　　허리띠 〔허리띠〕 **heoritti** *belt*

04 동사   dongsa   **Verbs**

옷(정장, 원피스, 상의, 하의)을/를 입다
〔오스립따/정장으립따/웜피스르립따/상이르립따/하이르립따〕
ot (jeongjang, wonpiseu, sangui, haui)eul/reul ipda
to wear clothing (suit, dress, top, bottoms)

장갑(반지)을 끼다 〔장가블끼다/반지를끼다〕 **janggap (banji)eul kkida**
to wear gloves (a ring)

모자를 쓰다 〔모자를쓰다〕 **mojareul sseuda** *to wear a hat*

양말(스타킹, 신발)을 신다 〔양마를신따/스타킹을신따/신바를신따〕
yangmal (seutaking, sinbal)eul sinda *to wear socks (stockings, shoes)*

목도리(스카프/액세서리)를 하다 〔목또리를하다/스카프를하다/액쎄서리를하다〕
mokdori (seukapeu/aekseseori)reul hada *to wear a muffler (scarf)/wear accessories*

넥타이를 매다 〔넥타이를매다〕 **nektaireul maeda** *to wear a necktie*

가방을 들다/메다 〔가방을들다/가방을메다〕 **gabangeul deulda/meda** *to carry a bag*

05 기타   gita   **Miscellaneous**

어울리다 〔어울리다〕 **eoullida** *to look good*

꽃무늬 〔꼰무니〕 **kkonmunui** *flower-print design*

물방울무늬 〔물빵울무니〕 **mulbangulmunui** *polka-dot pattern*

줄무늬 〔줄무니〕 **julmunui** *stripe*

발음규칙 Pronunciation Rules

'의' 의 발음 How to pronounce the vowel 의
When the vowel ㅢ follows a consonant (anything other than ㅇ), it is pronounced as ㅣ instead of ㅢ.

$$꽃무늬 \Rightarrow 〔꼰무니〕$$
$$ㄴ + ㅢ \Rightarrow 니$$

희망 히망 **huimang** *hope*
하늬바람 하니바람 **hanuibaram** *west wind*
띄어쓰기 띠어쓰기 **ttuieosseugi** *word spacing*

Grammar 문법

01 V- 고 있다 V-go itda

Am/are/is wearing

비비엔 씨는 빨간 원피스를 입고 있어요.

Situation

Vivien is wearing a red dress today. You say: 비비엔 씨는 빨간 원피스를 입고 있어요. She's also wearing a yellow hat. You say: 비비엔 씨는 노란 모자를 쓰고 있어요.

Explanation

The construction V-고 있다 is often used after a verb that indicates wearing something such as 입다 or 신다 or 쓰다 or 끼다 or 하다 or 매다. It tells us that the item of clothing is still being worn. In English, we can use the present continuous form "be V-ing" in this context, though it is also possible to use the preposition "in," as in "the woman in the blue dress."

리리 씨는 노란 원피스를 입고 있어요.
riri ssineun noran wonpiseureul ipgo isseoyo
Lili is wearing a yellow dress.

벤슨 씨는 파란 모자를 쓰고 있어요.
benseun ssineun paran mojareul sseugo isseoyo
Benson is wearing a blue hat.

스테파니 씨는 반지를 끼고 있어요.
seutepani ssineun banjireul kkigo isseoyo
Stephanie is wearing a ring.

■ **How to make** V-고 있다

Use V-고 있다 whether or not there is a final consonant in the last syllable of the verb stem.

Final Consonant + 고 있다: 입다 → 입다 + 고 있다 → 입고 있다

No Final Consonant + 고 있다: 끼다 → 끼다 + 고 있다 → 끼고 있다

활용 연습 1 Usage Practice 1

Fill in the blanks. Find the answers on page 257.

Base Form	V-고 있다
양복을 입다	양복을 입고 있다.
원피스를 입다	
모자를 쓰다	
구두를 신다	
넥타이를 매다	
반지를 끼다	반지를 끼고 있다.
팔찌를 하다	
장갑을 끼다	
목걸이를 하다	
안경을 쓰다	
가방을 들다	

02 V-는 N V-neun N   Who/which/that

Situation

That person is watching a movie. You say: 영화를 보는 사람.
That person is eating a banana. You say: 바나나를 먹는 사람.

Explanation

The V-는 N construction indicates that the action referred to
by a verb such as 보다 and 먹다 is taking place in the present.
It is used to modify the noun that follows it.

리리 씨는 저기에서 커피를 마시는 사람이에요.
riri ssineun jeogieseo keopireul masineun saramieyo
Lili is the person who is having coffee over there.

비비엔 씨는 빨간 원피스를 입고 있는 사람이에요.
bibien ssineun ppalgan wonpiseureul ipgo inneun saramieyo
Vivien is the person who is wearing a red dress.

지금은 숙제를 하는 시간이에요.
jigeumeun sukjereul haneun siganieyo
Now is the time to do my homework.

■ How to make V-는 N

Use V-는 N whether or not there is a final consonant in the last syllable of the verb stem.
When the final consonant is ㄹ, however, the ㄹ should be dropped from the V-는 N form.

Final Consonant + 는 N:
바나나를 먹다/사람 → 바나나를 먹다 + 는 사람 → 바나나를 먹는 사람

No Final Consonant + 는 N:
영화를 보다/사람 → 영화를 보다 + 는 사람 → 영화를 보는 사람

Final Consonant ㄹ → ㄹ + 는 N:
케이크를 만들다/시간 → 케이크를 만들다 + 는 시간 → 케이크를 만드는 시간

활용 연습 2 Usage Practice 2

Fill in the blanks. Find the answers on page 257.

Base Form	V-는 N
영화를 보다/사람	영화를 보는 사람
잠을 자다/시간	
마시다/커피	
좋아하다/운동	
못 먹다/음식	
일어나다/시간	
부산에 가다/버스	
호떡을 팔다/사람	

Conversation Practice 회화 연습

| 01 | 노란 원피스를 입고 있어요.
noran wonpiseureul ipgo isseoyo | (She) is wearing a yellow dress. |

Use the example sentences to guide you as you practice. Find model sentences on page 257.

가: 리리 씨가 누구예요?
riri ssiga nuguyeyo
Who is Lili?

나: 리리 씨는 노란 원피스를 입고 있어요.
riri ssineun noran wonpiseureul ipgo isseoyo
Lili is wearing a yellow dress.

. . . .

가: 스테파니 씨가, _____ ?

나: _____ .

. . . .

가: 아마니 씨가, _____ ?

나: _____ .

. . . .

가: 벤슨 씨가 _____ ?

나: _____ .

. . . .

가: 준이치 씨가 _____ ?

나: _____ .

. . . .

가: 하즈키 씨가 _____?

나: _____.

만들어 보세요.

가: _____?

나: _____.

02 리리 씨가 먹는 과일은 사과예요.   **The fruit that Lili is eating is an apple.**
riri ssiga meongneun gwaireun sagwayeyo

Use the example sentences to guide you as you practice. Find model sentences on page 257.

가: 리리 씨가 먹는 과일이 뭐예요?
riri ssiga meongneun gwairi mwoyeyo
What is the fruit that Lili is eating?

나: 리리 씨가 먹는 과일은 사과예요.
riri ssiga meongneun gwaireun sagwayeyo
The fruit that Lili is eating is an apple.

가: 스테파니 씨가 _____ 커피가 뭐예요?

나: _____ .

가: 벤슨 씨가 _____ ?

나: _____ .

가: 하즈키 씨가 _____ ?

나: _____ .

가: 비비엔 씨가 _____ ?

나: _____ .

음악
K-POP을
듣다

가: 앙리 씨가 _____?

나: _____ .

운동
골프를
좋아하다

가: 아마니 씨가 _____?

나: _____ .

만들어 보세요.

가: _____?

나: _____ .

(예)

광화문
이준기, 음식
보쌈을
먹다

청와대
이준기, 노래
*〈한마디만〉을
부르다

극장
이준기, 드라마
*〈아랑사또전〉을
촬영하다

* "Only One Word" is a
song by Lee Joon-gi.

* *Arang and the Magistrate*
is a TV drama that
starred Lee Joon-gi.

03 리리 씨가 먹는 사과는 맛있어요.
riri ssiga meongneun sagwaneun masisseoyo

The apple that Lili is eating is tasty.

Use the example sentences to guide you as you practice. Find model sentences on page 258.

기: 리리 씨가 먹는 사과는 어때요?
riri ssiga meongneun sagwaneun eottaeyo
What does the apple that Lili is eating taste like?

나: 리리 씨가 먹는 사과는 맛있어요.
riri ssiga meongneun sagwaneun masisseoyo
The apple that Lili is eating is delicious.

가: 스테파니 씨가 _____ 커피가 어때요?

나: _____ .

가: 비비엔 씨가 _____ ?

나: _____ .

가: 아마니 씨가 _____ ?

나: _____ .

가: 요나단 씨가 _____ ?

나: _____ .

책을 읽다
어렵다

가: 앙리 씨가 _____ ?

나: _____ .

김치찌개를 먹다
맵다

가: 퍼디 씨가 _____ ?

나: _____ .

만들어 보세요.

가: _____ ?

나: _____ .

예

광화문
이준기를
좋아하다
멋있다

청와대
이준기가
드라마를 촬영하다
재미있다

극장
이준기가
도시락을 먹다
맛있다

Listening Practice 1 　 듣기 연습 1

ONLINE AUDIO
05:35

Listen to the online audio, refer to the illustrations, and make a list of the names mentioned.
You can find the audio script on page 242.

문제 그림에 친구들의 이름을 쓰세요.

Listening Practice 2 　 듣기 연습 2

ONLINE AUDIO
07:31

Listen to the online audio, refer to the illustrations, and make a list of the names mentioned. You can find the audio script on page 242.

문제 그림에 친구들의 이름을 쓰세요.

Talking with Lee Joon-gi 이준기와 이야기하기

Try having a conversation with Lee Joon-gi as you listen to the audio. You can find a translation of this conversation on page 248.

하즈키   이 사람들은 모두 누구예요?

이준기   이 사람들은 모두 제 친구들이에요.

하즈키   우아! 여기 꽃무늬 원피스를 입고 있는 사람은 누구예요?

이준기   그 사람은 스테파니 씨예요.

하즈키   청바지를 입고 있고 빨간 티셔츠를 입고 있는 사람은 누구예요?

이준기   그 사람은 비비엔 씨예요. 청바지가 아주 잘 어울리지요?

하즈키   네. 여기 까만 양복을 입고 있는 사람은 누구예요?

이준기   안경을 쓰고 있는 사람요? 그 사람은 준이치 씨예요.

하즈키   아! 그런데 이준기 씨는 어디에 있어요?

이준기   저는 스테파니 씨 옆에 노란 티셔츠를 입고 있는 사람이에요.

하즈키   우아! 이준기 씨는 정말 멋있어요!

연습해 보기 1 Let's Practice 1

Use the example sentences to guide you as you practice. It's even more helpful to do this with a friend who is studying Korean.

최지영 스테파니 씨, 좋아하는 운동이 뭐예요?

스테파니 제가 좋아하는 운동은 요가예요.

질문 친구	1) 스테파니	2)	3)
1) 좋아하는 운동	요가		
2) 좋아하는 과일	바나나		
3) 못 먹는 음식	떡볶이		
4) 좋아하는 가수	지드래곤		
5) 싫어하는 계절	여름		

 Introduce your friends just as Jiyoung does.

최지영 스테파니 씨가 좋아하는 운동은 요가예요.
　　　　좋아하는 과일은 바나나예요.
　　　　그리고 못 먹는 음식은 떡볶이예요.
　　　　떡볶이는 매워서 못 먹어요.
　　　　그리고 좋아하는 가수는 지드래곤이에요.
　　　　싫어하는 계절은 여름이에요.

연습해 보기 2 Let's Practice 2

Find a picture of your friends and describe what they are wearing using the expression V-고 있는 사람 as in the example below.

친구들과 함께 찍은 사진을 찾아서 'V-고 있는 사람'을 사용해서 아래처럼 친구들의 옷차림을 설명하는 글을 써 보세요.

> 이 사람들은 모두 제 친구들이에요.
> 노란 원피스를 입고 있는 사람은 스테파니 씨예요.
> 그리고 . . .

_____

_____

_____

_____

_____

_____

_____

Lee Joon-gi's Guide to Korea

Korean Folk Village

Location for Historical Dramas and Films

"Mom, Dad, what was life like for people during the Joseon Dynasty?"

As I get ready to write about the Korean Folk Village, I can't help but think about the curious children wandering with their parents around the old buildings. The village recreates life at the end of the Joseon Dynasty in the nineteenth century, and it's common to see children and parents who have come to find out about the lives of their ancestors. This is just another example of how serious Korean parents are about ensuring that their children receive a good education.

The Korean Folk Village might look familiar to those who have watched Korean historical dramas. Most Korean historical movies or TV shows are filmed here. This makes it an especially meaningful place for me, as I have starred in quite a few such shows, from *The King and the Clown* to *Arang and the Magistrate*. The village is chock-full of memories for me.

With a number of events held here such as folk music performances, tightrope-walking competitions, and traditional weddings, you might feel like you've taken a step back in time. Take some photos with these scenes as the backdrop. Later, you'll be surprised to see yourself in such an unusual space. Surrounded by such exotic sights, your photos are sure to turn out well.

함께
떠나요!

The streets of the Korean Folk Village recreate the daily life of Joseon-era Korea.

Musicians are playing nongak, or "farmers' music," in the folk village.

Talking About Changes
달라진 것 이야기하기

날씨가
추워졌어요
The Weather
Has Gotten
Colder

Learning Objective

Situation
Talking about
changes
Vocabulary
Places
Physical appearance
Grammar
To become/get
Comparisons

ONLINE
AUDIO
00:10

퍼디 peodi	최지영 씨, 오늘 너무 춥지요? **choejiyeong ssi, oneul neomu chupjiyo** *Jiyoung, it's really cold today, isn't it?*
최지영 choejiyeong	네, 어제보다 많이 추워졌어요. **ne, eojeboda mani chuwojyeosseoyo** *Yeah, it's a lot colder than yesterday.*
퍼디 peodi	이럴 때 스키를 타면 좋겠어요. **ireol ttae seukireul tamyeon jokesseoyo** *At a time like this, it would be great to go skiing.*
최지영 choejiyeong	그럼, 이번 주말에 같이 스키를 타러 갈까요? **geureom, ibeon jumare gachi seukireul tareo galkkayo** *Well, why don't you go skiing with me this weekend?*
퍼디 peodi	네, 좋아요. 그런데 최지영 씨는 스키를 잘 타세요? **ne, joayo. geureonde choejiyeong ssineun seukireul jal taseyo** *Yeah, that sounds good. By the way, are you good at skiing?*
최지영 choejiyeong	아니요, 저는 무서워서 잘 못 타요. **aniyo, jeoneun museowoseo jal mot tayo** *No. It's too scary, so I'm not very good at it.*
퍼디 peodi	저도 어렸을 때는 무서워서 잘 못 탔지만 자꾸 타니까 실력이 늘었어요. **jeodo eoryeosseul ttaeneun museowoseo jal mot tatjiman jakku tanikka sillyeogi neureosseoyo** *When I was young, I was scared and couldn't ski very well, either.* *But since I kept skiing, I got a lot better.*
최지영 choejiyeong	그럼, 이번 주말에 퍼디 씨가 좀 가르쳐 주세요. **geureom, ibeon jumare peodi ssiga jom gareuchyeo juseyo** *In that case, can you show me how to ski this weekend?*
퍼디 peodi	네, 좋아요. **ne, joayo** *Sure.*

Vocabulary and Expressions 어휘와 표현

ONLINE AUDIO
02:14

01 장소 jangso — Places

빌딩 〔빌딩〕 **bilding** *building*

대형마트 〔대형마트〕 **daehyeongmateu** *supermarket*

레스토랑 〔레스토랑〕 **reseutorang** *restaurant (classy)*

체육관 〔체육꽌〕 **cheyukgwan** *gymnasium*

놀이터 〔노리터〕 **noriteo** *playground*

벼룩시장 〔벼룩씨장〕 **byeoruksijang** *flea market*

주점 〔주점〕 **jujeom** *pub*

길거리 〔길꺼리〕 **gilgeori** *street, road*

가게 〔가게〕 **gage** *store*

식당 〔식땅〕 **sikdang** *restaurant*

공터 〔공터〕 **gongteo** *vacant lot*

김밥집 〔김밥찝〕 **gimbapjip** *gimbap diner*

광장 〔광장〕 **gwangjang** *square, plaza*

노래방 〔노래방〕 **noraebang** *karaoke*

*북카페 〔북카페〕 **bukkape** *book café*

소극장 〔소극짱〕 **sogeukjang** *small theater*

*Book café: You'll find a lot of book cafés if you visit Korea. At these establishments, you can choose a book to browse as you drink your coffee.

02 형용사 hyeongyongsa — Adjectives

길다 〔길다〕 **gilda** *to be long*

복잡하다 〔복짜파다〕 **bokjapada** *to be complicated*

뚱뚱하다 〔뚱뚱하다〕 **ttungttunghada** *to be fat*

높다 〔놉따〕 **nopda** *to be high*

착하다 〔차카다〕 **chakada** *to be nice, to be kind*

남자답다 〔남자답따〕 **namjadapda** *to be manly, to be masculine*

실력이 늘다 〔실려기늘다〕 **sillyeogi neulda** *to get better at doing something*

짧다 〔짤따〕 **jjalda** *to be short*

어리다 〔어리다〕 **eorida** *to be young*

날씬하다 〔날씬하다〕 **nalssinhada** *to be skinny*

심심하다 〔심시마다〕 **simsimhada** *to be bored*

나쁘다 〔나쁘다〕 **nappeuda** *to be bad*

기분이 좋다/나쁘다 〔기부니조타/기부니나쁘다〕 **gibuni jota/nappeuda** *be in a good/bad mood*

매출이 늘다/줄다 〔매추리늘다/매추리줄다〕 **maechuri neulda/julda** *business sales increase/decrease*

03 동사 dongsa — Verbs

생기다 〔생기다〕 **saenggida** *to appear, to look like*

비교하다 〔비교하다〕 **bigyohada** *to compare*

수다를 떨다 〔수다를떨다〕 **sudareul tteolda** *to make small talk*

헤어지다 〔헤어지다〕 **heeojida** *to break up, to separate*

싸우다 〔싸우다〕 **ssauda** *to fight*

군대 가다 〔군대가다〕 **gundae gada** *to join the army*

04 기타 gita — Miscellaneous

이럴 때 〔이럴때〕 **ireol ttae** *at a time like this*

실력 〔실력〕 **sillyeok** *ability*

그대로 〔그대로〕 **geudaero** *as it is*

작년 〔장년〕 **jangnyeon** *last year*

도시 〔도시〕 **dosi** *city*

길 〔길〕 **gil** *road, way*

휴대폰 〔휴대폰〕 **hyudaepon** *mobile phone*

고향 〔고향〕 **gohyang** *one's hometown*

자꾸 〔자꾸〕 **jakku** *repeatedly, again and again*

많이 〔마니〕 **mani** *a lot*

올해 〔올해〕 **olhae** *this year*

교통 〔교통〕 **gyotong** *traffic*

자동차 〔자동차〕 **jadongcha** *automobile*

거리 〔거리〕 **geori** *street, distance*

공중전화 〔공중전화〕 **gongjungjeonhwa** *public payphone*

마을 〔마을〕 **maeul** *village, town*

발 음 규 칙 Pronunciation Rules

경음화 Tensification

When the initial sounds ㄱ, ㄷ, ㅂ, ㅅ or ㅈ come after final consonant ㅂ, they are pronounced as ㄲ, ㄸ, ㅃ, ㅆ and ㅉ respectively.

$$춥지요 \Rightarrow 〔춥찌요〕$$

$$ㅂ + ㅈ \Rightarrow ㅂ + ㅉ$$

맵고 맵꼬 **maepgo** *spicy and*

답답해요 답따패요 **dapdapaeyo** *I'm frustrated.*

밥상 밥쌍 **bapsang** *dining table*

답보 답뽀 **dapbo** *stalemate*

Grammar 문법

01 A- 아 / 어지다 A-a/eojida   **To become**

Situation

You were overweight so you worked out every day. You got thinner. You say: 날씬해졌어요. In winter it was cold but now that it's March the weather has become much warmer. You say: 날씨가 따뜻해졌어요.

Explanation

A-아/어지다 is a construction that can express a change in characteristics. In English, this is equivalent to the words "became" or "got," used in conjunction with adjectives.

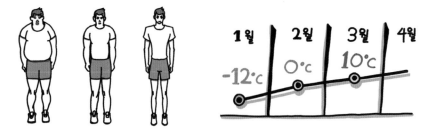

날씨가 추워졌어요.
nalssiga chuwojyeosseoyo
The weather has gotten cold.

리리 씨가 뚱뚱해졌어요.
riri ssiga ttungttunghaejyeosseoyo
Lili has gotten fat.

키가 커졌어요.
kiga keojyeosseoyo
(She/he) has grown tall.

■ How to make A-아/어지다

Use A-아지다 when the vowel in the final syllable of the adjective stem is ㅏ or ㅗ, and use A-어지다 when it is not.

ㅏ, ㅗ일 때 + 아지다: 많다 → 많다 + 아지다 → 많아지다

ㅏ ㅗ가 아닐 때 + 어지다: 재미있다 → 재미있다 + 어지다 → 재미있어지다

~하다 → ~해지다: 따뜻하다 → 따뜻하다 + 해지다 → 따뜻해지다

Final Consonant ㅂ → 우+어지다: 춥다 → 춥다 + 워(우 + 어)지다 → 추워지다

활용 연습 1 Usage Practice 1

Fill in the blanks. Find the answers on page 258.

Base Form	A-아/어졌어요	Base Form	A-아/어졌어요
많다	많아졌어요.	적다	
좋다		나쁘다	
키가 크다		길다	
날씬하다		뚱뚱하다	
따뜻하다		춥다	
작다		바쁘다	
*있다 → 생기다	생겼어요.	아름답다	

* For 있다, we don't say 있어졌어요. Instead, we say 생겼어요, which is the past tense of the verb 생기다.

02 N1 보다 N2 N1 boda N2 Comparisons

수박보다 사과가 더 좋아요.

Situation

If it's a choice between apples and watermelon, you prefer apples. You say: 수박보다 사과가 더 좋아요. Now that it's March the weather is warmer than in January. You say: 1월보다 (3월이) 따뜻해졌어요.

Explanation

The construction N1보다 N2 is used when comparing and evaluating two nouns like 사과 and 수박. We can say that compared to watermelons, apples are 더 좋다 or 더 맛있다 or 더 비싸다, and so on. 보다 is equivalent to "than" in English and it is placed after a noun with no space.

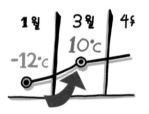

1월보다 따뜻해졌어요

어제보다 오늘이 더 추워졌어요.
eojeboda oneuri deo chuwojyeosseoyo
Today is colder than yesterday.

리리 씨보다 비비엔 씨가 더 날씬해요.
riri ssiboda bibien ssiga deo nalssinhaeyo
Vivien is slimmer than Lili.

아침보다 기분이 좋아졌어요.
achimboda gibuni joajyeosseoyo
I feel better than this morning.

■ How to make N1보다 N2

Use 보다 whether or not there is a final consonant in the last syllable of the noun.

Final Consonant + 보다: 수박/사과 → 수박보다 사과

No Final Consonant + 보다: 커피/맥주 → 커피보다 맥주

활용 연습 2 Usage Practice 2

Fill in the blanks. Find the answers on page 258.

Base Form	N1보다 N2
노래방/광장	노래방보다 광장
길거리/소극장	
주점/북카페	

03 A/V-(으) ㄹ 때 , A/V- 았 / 었을 때
A/V-(eu)r ttae, A/V-at/eosseul ttae

When

Situation

You eat popcorn when you watch movies. You say: 영화를 볼 때 팝콘을 먹어요. When you were young, you went swimming in the ocean." You say: 어렸을 때 바다에서 수영했어요.

Explanation

A/V-(으)ㄹ 때 and A/V-았/었을 때 indicate the timeframe of an adjective such as 어리다 or a verb like 영화를 보다. The construction A/V-(으)ㄹ 때 can refer either to the present or to what usually happens, while A/V-았/었을 때 is used when talking about the past. In English, the equivalent construction is a "when" clause, with the tense expressed in the main verb of the clause. See the example sentences on the next page.

저는 영화를 볼 때 팝콘을 먹어요.

jeoneun yeonghwareul bol ttae papkoneul meogeoyo

I eat popcorn when watching a movie.

저는 기분이 나쁠 때 잠을 자요.

jeoneun gibuni nappeul ttae jameul jayo

I sleep when I feel bad.

저는 어렸을 때 친구들과 바다에서 수영했어요.

jeoneun eoryeosseul ttae chingudeulgwa badaeseo suyeonghaesseoyo

I swam in the sea with my friends when I was young.

지난주에 친구를 만났을 때 같이 수다를 떨었어요.

jinanjue chingureul mannasseul ttae gachi sudareul tteoreosseoyo

When I met my friends last week, I had a chat with them.

■ How to make A/V-(으)ㄹ 때

Use A/V-을 때 when there is a final consonant in the last syllable of the verb or adjective stem and use A/V-ㄹ 때 when there is not.

Final Consonant + 을 때: 많다 → 많다 + 을 때 → 많을 때

No Final Consonant + ㄹ 때: 커피를 마시다 → 커피를 마시다 + ㄹ 때 → 커피를 마실 때

Final Consonant ㄹ → ㄹ + ㄹ 때: 만들다 → 만들다 + ㄹ 때 → 만들 때

Final Consonant ㄷ → ㄹ + 을 때 : 음악을 듣다 → 음악을 듣다 + ㄹ 을 때 → 음악을 들을 때

Final Consonant ㅂ → 우 +ㄹ 때: 춥다 → 춥다 + 울 (우+ㄹ) 때 → 추울 때

■ How to make A/V-았/었을 때

Use A/V-았을 때 when the vowel in the final syllable of the adjective or verb stem is ㅏ or ㅗ and use A/V-었을 때 when it is not.

ㅏ, ㅗ일 때 + 았을 때: 좋다 → 좋다 + 았을 때 → 좋았을 때

ㅏ, ㅗ가 아닐 때 + 었을 때: 읽다 → 읽다 + 었을 때 → 읽었을 때

~하다 → ~했을 때: 여행하다 → 여행하다 + 했을 때 → 여행했을 때

ㅣ → 였을 때: 어리다 → 어리다 + 였을 때 → 어렸을 때

Final Consonant ㅂ → 우 + 었을 때: 덥다 → 덥다 + 웠 (우+었)을 때 → 더웠을 때

활용 연습 3 Usage Practice 3

Fill in the blanks. Find the answers on page 258.

Base Form	A/V-(으)ㄹ 때	A/V-았/었을 때
어리다	어릴 때	어렸을 때
영화를 보다		
친구를 만나다		
기분이 나쁘다		
시간이 많다		
돈이 없다		
고등학교에 다니다		
피자를 먹다		
여자 친구와 헤어지다		
남자 친구와 싸우다		
수업을 하다		
떡볶이가 맵다		
길을 걷다		
꽃을 팔다		

Conversation Practice 회화 연습

01	리리 씨가 작년보다 뚱뚱해졌어요 . riri ssiga jangnyeonboda ttungttunghaejyeosseoyo	**Lili has gotten fat compared to last year.**

Use the example sentences to guide you as you practice. Find model sentences on page 258.

리리
작년
뚱뚱하다

가: 리리 씨가 어때요?
riri ssiga eottaeyo
How is Lili?

나: 리리 씨가 작년보다 뚱뚱해졌어요.
riri ssiga jangnyeonboda ttungttunghaejyeosseoyo
She has gotten fat compared to last year.

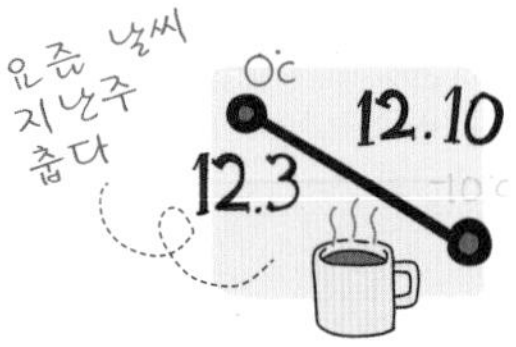

요즘 날씨
지난주
춥다
Oᵒc 12.10 12.3

가: _____ 이/가 어때요?

나: _____ .

한국의 교통
5년 전
복잡하다

가: _____ ?

나: _____ .

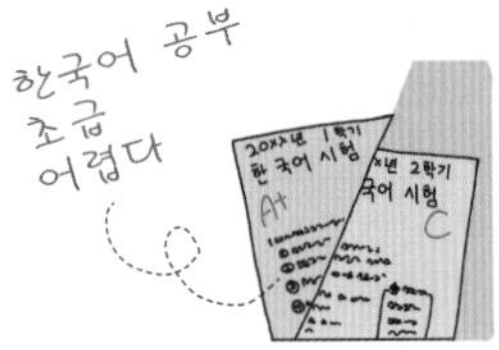

한국어 공부
초급
어렵다

가: _____ ?

나: _____ .

지금 기분
밤
좋다

가: _____ ?

나: _____ .

요즘 하즈키
한달 전
날씬하다

가: _____ ?

나: _____ .

만들어 보세요.

가: _____ ?

나: _____ .

예

이준기
군대 가기 전
남자답다

하즈키
작년
한국 친구가 많다

아마니 씨 동생
6개월 전
키가 크다

비비엔
한달 전
태권도 실력이 좋다

학교 앞
작년
복잡하다

02 기분이 나쁠 때 잠을 자요.
gibuni nappeul ttae jameul jayo

I sleep when I feel bad.

Use the example sentences to guide you as you practice. Find model sentences on page 258.

기분이 나쁘다
잠을 자다

가: 스테파니 씨, 기분이 나쁠 때 보통 뭐 해요?
seutepani ssi, gibuni nappeul ttae botong mwo haeyo
Stephanie, what do you usually do when you feel bad?

나: 저는 기분이 나쁠 때 보통 잠을 자요.
jeoneun gibuni nappeul ttae botong jameul jayo
I usually sleep when I feel bad.

영화를 보다
팝콘을 먹다

가: 비비엔 씨, _____ ?

나: _____ .

피곤하다
샤워하다

가: 이준기 씨, _____ ?

나: _____ .

기분이 좋다
친구를 만나다

가: 요나단 씨, _____ ?

나: _____ .

만들어 보세요.
신신하다
기분이 나쁘다
친구에게 전화하다
음악을 듣다
...

가: _____ ?

나: _____ .

03 어렸을 때 바다에서 수영했어요.
eoryeosseul ttae badaeseo suyeonghaesseoyo

I swam in the sea when I was young.

Use the example sentences to guide you as you practice. Find model sentences on page 258.

어렸다
바다에서 수영했다

가: 요나단 씨, 어렸을 때 보통 뭐 했어요?
yonadan ssi, eoryeosseul ttae botong mwo haesseoyo
Jonathan, what did you usually do when you were young?

나: 저는 어렸을 때 보통 바다에서 수영했어요.
jeoneun eoryeosseul ttae botong badaeseo suyeonghaesseoyo
I usually swam in the sea when I was young.

술을 마셨다
노래를 했다

가: 비비엔 씨, _____ ?

나: 저는 _____ .

기분이 나빴다 먹었다
맛있는 음식을

가: 이준기 씨, _____ ?

나: _____ .

친구를 만났다
영화를 봤다

가: 퍼디 씨, _____ ?

나: _____ .

만들어 보세요

시험을 잘 봤다
남자 친구와 헤어졌다
맛있는 음식을 먹었다
여행을 갔다
...

가: _____ ?

나: _____ .

Listening Practice 듣기 연습

ONLINE AUDIO
05:29

Listen to the audio and decide which picture most closely matches the description you hear. You can find the audio script on page 242.

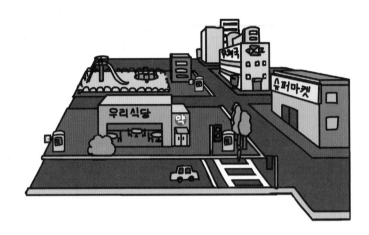

문제 이 도시가 변한 모습과 같은 것을 고르세요.

그림 1

그림 2

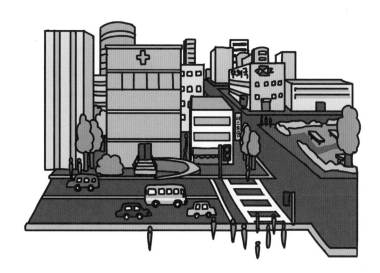

그림 3

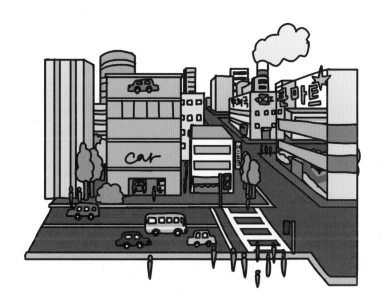

Talking with Lee Joon-gi 이준기와 이야기하기

ONLINE AUDIO
07:45

Listen to Lee Joon-gi talk about his home town, then do the exercise on the facing page. You can find a translation of this conversation on page 248.

이준기

여러분 안녕하세요? 이준기예요. 여기는 제 고향이에요.

지금 제 고향은 아주 복잡해요. 그렇지만 10년 전에는 복잡하지 않았어요.

10년 전과 비교하면 아주 복잡해졌어요. 자동차도 10년 전보다 많아졌어요.

그래서 길도 넓어졌어요. 그리고 높은 빌딩도 많이 생겼어요.

10년 전에는 약국이 있었지만 지금은 없어지고 병원이 생겼어요.

작은 가게가 없어지고 대형마트가 생겼어요. 빌딩 3층에는 큰 레스토랑이

생겼어요. 어렸을 때 저는 마을 앞에 있는 공터에서 친구들과 농구를 했어요.

하지만 지금은 그 공터에 체육관이 생겼어요. 거리에 사람들도 많아졌어요.

사람들이 모두 휴대폰을 사용해서 공중전화도 없어졌어요.

하지만 우체국과 김밥집은 그대로 있어요.

연습해 보기 1 Let's Practice 1

Use this page to write a description of a place you know that has changed. You can draw a picture too if you want. Try to use some of the structures that Lee Joon-gi uses in his description.

여러분이 아는 장소 중 과거와 현재의 모습이 많이 달라진 곳이 있습니까? 그곳이 어떻게 달라졌는지 '-아/어지다'와 '-보다'를 사용해서 비교하는 글을 쓰세요. 원하면 그림도 그리세요.

연습해 보기 2 Let's Practice 2

Fill in the chart with your ideas and then create a conversation between Jiyoung and friends as the example shown below.

최지영   스테파니 씨, 기분이 나쁠 때 보통 뭐 해요?
스테파니 저는 기분이 나쁠 때 재미있는 영화를 봐요.
최지영   어렸을 때 보통 뭐 했어요?
스테파니 어렸을 때 보통 바다에서 수영했어요.

친구 \ 질문	기분이 나쁠 때 보통 뭐 해요?	어렸을 때 보통 뭐 했어요?
1) 스테파니	재미있는 영화를 보다	바다에서 수영하다
2)		
3)		

Pyeongchang

Film Location of the movie *Welcome to Dongmakgol* and Site of the 2018 Winter Olympics

Have you seen the movie *Welcome to Dongmakgol*? This enchanting movie, which is memorable for its snowy landscapes, portrays the simple country life of the people of Gangwon Province. The film was shot in the province's Dongmak Valley, in the region of Pyeongchang.

Gangwon Province is a mountainous part of Korea. In the winter, Pyeongchang draws skiers with its snow-covered slopes, while in the other seasons the green fields resemble pastures high in the Alps. Nowadays, Pyeongchang makes many Korean people think of the 2018 Winter Olympics and figure skater Kim Yu-Na. This is because Kim Yu-Na worked hard to help Pyeongchang win the bid for the winter Olympics.

In the past, winter sports were not very popular in Korea. Today, however, you often see people going skiing, learning to snowboard, or enjoying other cold-weather activities. To all of you out there who are pursuing your dreams on the fields of snow, I'm cheering for you!

함께
떠나요!

Each winter,
skiers are drawn to the snowy slopes.

The film set of *Welcome to Dongmakgol*.
The movie is memorable for shots of falling snow.

Expressing What You Can Do

할 수 있는 것 말하기

Learning Objective

Situation
Expressing what
you can do
Vocabulary
Food
Flavors
Activities
Grammar
Can/can't
Unable to

ONLINE
AUDIO
00:10

앙리 angni	최지영 씨, 오늘 시간이 있어요? **choejiyeong ssi, oneul sigani isseoyo** *Jiyoung, are you free today?*	
최지영 choejiyeong	네, 있어요. **ne, isseoyo** *Yes, I am.*	
앙리 angni	그럼, 같이 점심을 먹을까요? **geureom, gachi jeomsimeul meogeulkkayo** *In that case, how about having lunch together?*	
최지영 choejiyeong	네, 좋아요. 무슨 음식을 먹을까요? **ne, joayo. museun eumsigeul meogeulkkayo** *Sure. What kind of food should we have?*	
앙리 angni	최지영 씨, 매운 음식을 먹을 수 있어요? **choejiyeong ssi, maeun eumsigeul meogeul su isseoyo** *Can you eat spicy food?*	
최지영 choejiyeong	아니요, 저는 매운 음식을 못 먹어요. 앙리 씨는요? **aniyo, jeoneun maeun eumsigeul mot meogeoyo. angni ssineunyo** *No. I can't eat spicy food. What about you?*	
앙리 angni	저는 먹을 수 있어요. 매운 음식을 아주 좋아해요. 그럼, 최지영 씨, 삼계탕을 먹을 수 있어요? **jeoneun meogeul su isseoyo. maeun eumsigeul aju joahaeyo. geureom, choejiyeong ssi, samgyetangeul meogeul su isseoyo** *I can eat it. I really like spicy food. Well, can you eat samgyetang?*	
최지영 choejiyeong	네, 아주 좋아해요. **ne, aju joahaeyo** *Yes, I really like it.*	
앙리 angni	그럼, 우리 삼계탕을 먹으러 갑시다. **geureom, uri samgyetangeul meogeureo gapsida** *OK, let's go eat some samgyetang.*	

Vocabulary and Expressions 어휘와 표현

ONLINE AUDIO
02:11

01 음식 eumsik   Foods

삼계탕 〔삼계탕/삼게탕〕 **samgyetang** *samgyetang (chicken soup)*

감자탕 〔감자탕〕 **gamjatang** *gamjatang (potato and pork bone stew)*

생선회 〔생선회〕 **saengseonhoe** *sashimi*   냉면 〔냉면〕 **naengmyeon** *naengmyeon noodles*

칼국수 〔칼국쑤〕 **kalguksu** *kalguksu noodles*   쫄면 〔쫄면〕 **jjolmyeon** *jjolmyeon noodles*

부대찌개 〔부대찌개〕 **budaejjigae** *budae jjigae (army base stew)*

닭갈비 〔닥깔비〕 **dakgalbi** *dalkgalbi (pan-fried chicken)*

찜닭 〔찜닥〕 **jjimdak** *steamed chicken*   김치 〔김치〕 **gimchi** *kimchi*

소주 〔소주〕 **soju** *soju*   소고기 〔소고기〕 **sogogi** *beef*

돼지고기 〔돼지고기〕 **dwaejigogi** *pork*   막걸리 〔막껄리〕 **makgeolli** *makgeolli*

02 형용사 (맛) hyeongyongsa (mat)   Adjectives (Flavors)

맵다 〔맵따〕 **maepda** *to be spicy*   짜다 〔짜다〕 **jjada** *to be salty*

싱겁다 〔싱겁따〕 **singgeopda** *to be bland*   쓰다 〔쓰다〕 **sseuda** *to be bitter*

달다 〔달다〕 **dalda** *to be sweet*   시다 〔시다〕 **sida** *to be sour*

떫다 〔떨따〕 **tteolda** *to be bitter*   고소하다 〔고소하다〕 **gosohada** *to be savory*

새콤하다 〔새콤하다〕 **saekomhada**   매콤하다 〔매콤하다〕 **maekomhada**
  to be tart   *to be a little hot*

달콤하다 〔달콤하다〕 **dalkomhada**   담백하다 〔담배카다〕 **dambaekada**
  to be sweet   *to be mild*

03 동사 dongsa   Verbs

운전하다 〔운전하다〕 **unjeonhada** *to drive*

촬영하다 〔촬령하다〕 **chwaryeonghada** *to shoot (a movie)*

담배를 피우다 〔담배를피우다〕 **dambaereul piuda** *to smoke a cigarette*

사진을 찍다 〔사지늘찍다〕 **sajineul jjikda** *to take a picture*

등산을 하다 〔등사늘하다〕 **deungsaneul hada** *to go hiking*

빵을 굽다 〔빵을굽다〕 **ppangeul gupda** *to bake bread*

04 기타 gita   **Miscellaneous**

부럽다 〔부럽따〕 **bureopda** *to be jealous, to be envious*

어깨를 주무르다 〔어깨를주무르다〕 **eokkaereul jumureuda** *to massage someone's shoulders*

깜짝 놀라다 〔깜짱놀라다〕 **kkamjjak nollada** *to be surprised*

가볍다 〔가볍따〕 **gabyeopda** *to be light (as in not heavy)*

아름답다 〔아름답따〕 **areumdapda** *to be beautiful*

행복하다 〔행보카다〕 **haengbokada** *to be happy*

제주도 〔제주도〕 **jejudo** *Jeju Island*

한라산 〔할라산〕 **hallasan** *Hallasan Mountain*

투명인간 〔투명잉간〕 **tumyeongingan** *someone who is invisible*

영화사 〔영화사〕 **yeonghwasa** *film studio*

스태프〔스태프〕 **seutaepeu** *staff*

카메라 〔카메라〕 **kamera** *camera*

살짝 〔살짝〕 **saljjak** *slightly, just a little, secretly*

공짜 〔공짜〕 **gongjja** *free, to cost nothing*

기숙사 〔기숙싸〕 **gisuksa** *dormitory*

발음규칙 Pronunciation Rules

경음화 Tensification
When the first syllable after a verb or adjective that ends with (으)ㄹ begins with ㄱ, ㄷ, ㅂ, ㅅ or ㅈ, that initial sound is pronounced as ㄲ, ㄸ, ㅃ, ㅆ, ㅉ.

$$\text{먹(을) 수 있어요} \Rightarrow \text{[머글쑤있어요]}$$
$$\text{(으)ㄹ} + \text{ㅅ} \Rightarrow \text{(으)ㄹ} + \text{ㅆ}$$

볼 수 있어요 볼쑤있어요 **bol su isseoyo** *can see*
갈 거예요 갈꺼예요 **gal geoyeyo** *will go*
할게 할께 **halge** *I will do*

Grammar 문법

01 V-(으)ㄹ 수 있다 / 없다   V-(eu)r su itda/eopda   Can/can't

Situation

You have a driver's license and you know how to drive. You say: 저는 운전할 수 있어요. You don't have a driver's license and you don't know how to drive. You say: 저는 운전할 수 없어요.

Explanation

The construction V-(으)ㄹ 수 있다 shows that you have the ability to perform the action of a verb such as 운전하다. In contrast, V-(으)ㄹ 수 없다 shows that you don't have that ability. In English, V-(으)ㄹ 수 있다 is expressed with "can V," while V-(으)ㄹ 수 없다 is expressed with "cannot V."

리리 씨, 피아노를 칠 수 있어요?
riri ssi, pianoreul chil su isseoyo
Lili, can you play the piano?

저는 번지점프를 할 수 있어요.
jeoneun beonjijeompeureul hal su isseoyo
I can do bungee jumping.

저는 매운 음식을 먹을 수 없어요.
jeoneun maeun eumsigeul meogeul su eopseoyo
I can't eat spicy food.

■ **How to make** V-(으)ㄹ 수 있다/V-(으)ㄹ 수 없다

A/V-을 수 있다/없다 is used when there is a final consonant in the last syllable of the stem, while A/V-ㄹ 수 있다/없다 is used when there is not.

Final Consonant + 을 수 있다/없다:
먹다 → 먹다 + 을 수 있다/없다 → 먹을 수 있다 / 먹을 수 없다

No Final Consonant + ㄹ 수 있다/없다:
만나다 → 만나다 + ㄹ 수 있다/없다 → 만날 수 있다 / 만날 수 없다

Final Consonant ㄹ → ㄹ + ㄹ 수 있다/없다:
만들다 → 만들다 + ㄹ 수 있다/없다 → 만들 수 있다 / 만들 수 없다

Final Consonant ㄷ → ㄹ+을 수 있다/없다:
듣다 → 듣다 + ㄹ을 수 있다/없다 → 들을 수 있다 / 들을 수 없다

Final Consonant ㅂ → 우 + ㄹ 수 있다/없다
춥다 → 춥다 + 울(우 + ㄹ) 수 있다/없다 → 추울 수 있다 / 추울 수 없다

활용 연습 1 Usage Practice 1

Fill in the blanks. Find the answers on page 259.

Base Form	V-(으)ㄹ 수 있어요	V-(으)ㄹ 수 없어요
자전거를 타다	자전거를 탈 수 있어요.	자전거를 탈 수 없어요.
번지점프를 하다		
삼계탕을 먹다		
소주를 마시다		
기숙사에 살다		
태권도를 하다		

02 못 / 안 V- 아 / 어요 mot/an V-a/eoyo

Unable to

Situation

You want to drive, but you don't have a driver's license. You say: 저는 운전을 못 해요. This means the same thing as 저는 운전을 할 수 없어요. But if you have a driver's license and you are not driving because you don't want to, you say: 저는 오늘 운전을 안 해요.

Explanation

The construction 못 V-아/어요 is used to say you cannot do something, while 안 V-아/어요 is used when you aren't doing something because you don't want to. 못 V-아/어요 is expressed with "cannot" in English, and 안 V-아/어요 is expressed with "do not."

저는 매운 음식을 못 먹어요.
jeoneun maeun eumsigeul mot meogeoyo
I can't eat spicy foods.

이번 방학에 고향에 못 가요.
ibeon banghage gohyange mot gayo
I can't visit my hometown during this vacation.

저는 담배를 안 피워요.
jeoneun dambaereul an piwoyo
I don't smoke.

■ How to make 못 V-아/어요, 안 V-아/어요

The 못 and 안 in these two constructions are used in front of the verb that they modify. With verbs that are made up of a noun plus 하다 such as 운전하다, 못 or 안 are placed between the noun and 하다.

보다: 못 봐요. 안 봐요.

먹다: 못 먹어요. 안 먹어요.

공부하다: 공부 못 해요. 공부 안 해요.

활용 연습 2 Usage Practice 2

Fill in the blanks. Find the answers on page 259.

Base Form	못 V-아/어요	안 V-아/어요
그림을 그리다	그림을 못 그려요.	그림을 안 그려요.
번지점프를 하다		
삼계탕을 먹다		
케이크를 만들다		
매운 음식을 먹다		
피아노를 치다		
소주를 마시다		
사진을 찍다		
운전하다		
태권도를 하다		

Conversation Practice 회화 연습

01 운전을 할 수 있어요.   **unjeoneul hal su isseoyo**   **(She/he) can drive.**

Use the example sentences to guide you as you practice. Find model sentences on page 259.

하즈키
운전을 하다

가: 하즈키 씨, 운전을 할 수 있어요?
hajeuki ssi, unjeoneul hal su isseoyo
Hazuki, can you drive?

나: 네, 저는 운전을 할 수 있어요.
ne, jeoneun unjeoneul hal su isseoyo
Yes, I can.

. . . .

가: 리리 씨, _____?

나: _____.

. . . .

가: 비비엔 씨, _____?

나: _____.

. . . .

가: 요나단 씨, _____?

나: _____.

. . . .

가: 최지영 씨, _____?

나: _____.

. . . .

가: 앙리 씨, _____ ?

나: _____ .

만들어 보세요.

가: _____ ?

나: _____ .

02 번지점프를 못 해요.
beonjijeompeureul mot haeyo

(She/he) can't do bungee jumping.

Use the example sentences to guide you as you practice. Find model sentences on page 259.

리리
번지점프를 하다

가: 리리 씨, 번지점프를 할 수 있어요?
riri ssi, beonjijeompeureul hal su isseoyo
Lili, can you do bungee jumping?

나: 아니요, 저는 번지점프를 못 해요.
aniyo, jeoneun beonjijeompeureul mot haeyo
No, I can't.

가: 하즈키 씨, _____ ?

나: 아니요, _____ .

가: 벤슨 씨, _____ ?

나: _____ .

가: 리리 씨, _____ ?

나: _____ .

가: 퍼디 씨, _____ ?

나: _____ .

가: 최지영 씨, _____?

나: _____.

만들어 보세요.

가: _____?

나: _____.

Listening Practice 듣기 연습

ONLINE AUDIO
05:14

Listen to two people talking about their upcoming vacation. In question 1, write the numbers of the activities they can do together. In question 2, write the numbers of the activities they can't do together. You can find the audio script on page 243.

문제 1   이번 방학에 두 사람이 같이 할 수 있는 것을 그림을 보고 고르세요.

문제 2   이번 방학에 두 사람이 같이 할 수 없는 것을 그림을 보고 고르세요.

Talking with Lee Joon-gi 1   이준기와 이야기하기 1

ONLINE AUDIO
07:56

Listen to Lee Joon-gi and Vivien (on the next page) talking about their day. Try listening without looking at the script first and test your comprehension. You can find a translation of these texts on page 249.

이준기   여러분 안녕하세요? 이준기예요.

저는 오늘 하루 동안 투명인간이 되었어요.

아침에 샤워를 안 하고 영화사에 갔어요.

저는 다른 배우들과 스태프들을 볼 수 있지만

그 사람들은 저를 볼 수 없어요.

그래서 쉬는 시간에는 카메라 감독님의 카메라를

살짝 들어 드리고 어깨를 주물러 드렸어요.

감독님이 깜짝 놀랐지만 기분이 좋아졌을 거예요.

오후에는 공짜로 비행기를 타고 시드니에 갔어요.

한국은 겨울이지만 시드니는 지금 여름이에요.

그래서 바다에서 수영했어요.

오늘은 모든 것을 할 수 있는 하루였어요.

그래서 참 행복했어요.

비비엔   여러분 안녕하세요? 비비엔이에요.

저는 오늘 하루 동안 투명인간이 되었어요.

아침에 학교에 갔어요.

저는 선생님과 친구들을 볼 수 있지만 선생님과 친구들은

저를 못 봐요.

그래서 리리 씨의 빵과 퍼디 씨의 바나나를 살짝 먹었어요.

리리 씨와 퍼디 씨는 빵과 바나나가 없어져서 깜짝 놀랐어요.

그리고 로이 씨의 커피도 마실 수 있었어요.

로이 씨도 커피가 없어져서 깜짝 놀랐어요.

그리고 수업이 끝나고 선생님의 가방을 살짝 들어 드렸어요.

선생님께서 "어! 오늘은 가방이 가볍다!" 라고 말했어요.

아마 선생님의 기분이 좋아졌을 거예요.

그래서 저도 기분이 좋은 하루였어요.

연습해 보기 Let's Practice

Fill in the chart with O and X with your ideas about what Jiyoung's friends can and can't do. Then create a conversation between Jiyoung and her friends following the example below.

최지영	스테파니 씨, 태권도를 할 수 있어요?
스테파니	네, 저는 태권도를 할 수 있어요.
최지영	번지점프를 할 수 있어요?
최지영	아니요, 저는 번지점프를 못 해요.

질문 　　　　　　　친구	1) 스테파니	2)	3)
1) 태권도를 하다	○		
2) 번지점프를 하다	×		
3) 김치를 담그다			
4) 스키를 타다			
5) 운전을 하다			

Daejeon

City of the Young Scientists

The city of Daejeon is home to scientific research complexes, including KAIST (Korea Advanced Institute of Science and Technology). It's at this university that some of Korea's most brilliant minds are gathered. These young students spend more time in the future than the present, dreaming up as many ideas as there are stars in the sky over Daejeon's Yuseong district, where the university is located.

Sometimes I ask myself whether scientific advances really benefit mankind. It's a challenging question, to be sure, one that each of you must answer for yourself! One thing is sure, though—there are no limits to the human imagination. We are living in the digital revolution, when all of our paradigms are shifting, and it's exciting to think about how our lives may be changed by what these scientists are dreaming of. Close to the Daedeok Research Complex are the Yuseong Hot Springs. Stop by the springs after a tiring day and let the hot water wash away your fatigue.

함께 떠나요!

Daejeon's Yuseong district is the site of a scientific research complex.

KAIST is home to some of Korea's most brilliant minds.

APPENDIX

Answer Key for Listening Practice
Translation of Talking with Lee Joon-gi
Answers to the Exercises
Vocabulary Index

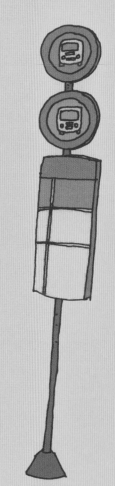

Answer Key for Listening Practice

Lesson 1: online audio file 05:39

요나단: 스테파니 씨, 이것은 무슨 사진이에요?
스테파니: 우리 가족 사진이에요.
요나단: 이분은 누구세요?
스테파니: 이분은 우리 아버지예요.
요나단: 아! 아버지는 무엇을 하세요?
스테파니: 우리 아버지는 의사예요.
　　　　　병원에서 일하세요.
요나단: 그래요! 이분은 어머니세요?
스테파니: 네, 우리 어머니예요.
요나단: 어머니는 뭐 하세요?
스테파니: 어머니는 요리사예요.
　　　　　호텔 레스토랑에서 일하세요.
요나단: 이 사람은 남동생이에요?
스테파니: 네, 제 동생은 중학생이에요.
　　　　　시드니 중학교에 다녀요.
　　　　　그리고 저는 대학생이에요.
　　　　　한국대학교에 다녀요.

<정답>

아버지:　의사
어머니:　요리사
스테파니:　대학생
남동생:　중학생

Lesson 2: online audio file 04:59

1) 앙리: 스테파니 씨는 어떤 사람이에요?
　비비엔: 스테파니 씨는 키가 작고 뚱뚱한
　　　　　사람이에요. 밥도 잘먹고 노래도
　　　　　잘하고 아주 귀여운 여자예요.
　앙리: 아, 그래요? 저는 노래를 잘하는 사람을
　　　　좋아해요. 한번 만나고 싶어요.

2) 비비엔: 준이치 씨는 어떤 사람이에요?

앙리: 제 친구 준이치 씨는 키가 크고 축구를
　　　좋아하는 사람이에요. 그래서 주말에는
　　　친구들과 같이 축구를 해요.
　　　그리고 준이치 씨는 얼굴도 잘생기고
　　　아주 친절한 사람이에요.
　　　그래서 친구들에게도 인기가 많아요.

3) 비비엔: 리리 씨는 어떤 사람이에요?
　앙리: 리리 씨는 키는 크지 않지만,
　　　　날씬하고 아주 예쁜 사람이에요. 그리고
　　　　조용하고 그림을 잘 그리는 사람이에요.
　　　　또 리리 씨는 여행을 좋아해요. 그래서
　　　　주말에는 보통 친구들과 같이 여행을
　　　　가요.

Lesson 3: online audio file 05:08

퍼디: 리리 씨, 방학을 하면 뭐 할 거예요?
리리　저는 방학을 하면 베이징에 갈 거예요.
퍼디: 우아! 부러워요. 베이징에 가면 뭐 할 거예요?
리리　베이징에 가면 친구를 만날 거예요.
　　　친구와 같이 이화원에 가고 베이징카오야를
　　　먹을 거예요.
　　　저는 베이징카오야를 아주 좋아해요.
퍼디: 아, 그래요?
리리　퍼디 씨는 방학을 하면 뭐 할 거예요?
퍼디: 저는 방학을 하면 아무것도 안 할 거예요.
리리　어! 퍼디 씨는 여행 안 갈 거예요?
퍼디: 네, 그냥 집에서 푹 쉴 거예요.
　　　집에서 늦잠도 자고, 가끔 등산도 할 거예요.
리리　아이고!
퍼디: 리리 씨, 베이징에서 예쁜 선물 사 오세요.
리리　네, 퍼디 씨도 잘 지내세요. 다음 학기에
　　　만나요.

<정답>
문제 1: ②, ④
문제 2: ⑤, ⑥

Lesson 4: online audio file 05:41

안녕하세요? 저는 스테파니예요.
지금 한국대학교에서 한국어를 공부하고 있어요.
다음 주에 TOPIK 시험이 있어요. 그래서 요즘
열심히 시험공부를 하고 있어요. 시험이 끝나면
친구들과 같이 바다에 갈 거예요. 바다에 가서
수영하고 싶어요. 그리고 태권도도 배우고 싶어요.
저는 대학교를 졸업하면 시드니에 가서
한국어 선생님이 되고 싶어요. 그리고 멋있는
남자 친구랑 결혼하고 싶어요.

<정답>
문제 1: ④, ⑥
문제 2: ②, ③

Lesson 5: Practice 1. Online audio file 05:03

듣기 연습 1
요나단: 실례합니다. 말씀 좀 묻겠습니다.
아주머니: 네, 말씀하세요.
요나단: 지하철을 타고 싶은데 이 근처에
            지하철역이 있어요?
아주머니: 네, 저기 보이는 육교를 건너서 100
            미터쯤 가면 지하도가 있어요. 지하도를
            건너서 왼쪽으로 가면 주유소가 보여요.
            지하철역은 주유소 뒤에 있어요.
요나단: 네, 알겠습니다. 감사합니다.

<정답> ⓓ

Lesson 5: Practice 2. Online audio file 06:27

듣기 연습 2
리리: 실례합니다. 커피숍이 어디예요?
직원: 저기 보이는 건물이 은행이에요.
리리: 네.

직원: 은행 옆길로 똑바로 올라가면 은행 뒤에 보이는
      빨간 벽돌 건물이 있어요.
      커피숍은 그 건물 4층에 있습니다.
리리: 네, 알겠습니다. 감사합니다.

<정답>
ⓓ

Lesson 6: Practice 1: Online audio file 04:18

듣기 연습 1
1) 리리

기사: 어서 오세요. 손님, 어디로 갈까요?
리리: 인사동으로 가 주세요.
      네, 알겠습니다.
      여기에서 인사동까지 얼마나 걸려요?
      지금은 길이 안 막힐 테니까 30분쯤
      걸릴 거예요.

2) 비비엔
기사: 어서 오세요. 손님, 어디로 갈까요?
비비엔: 교보문고로 가 주세요.
기사: 네, 알겠습니다.
비비엔: 여기에서 교보문고까지 얼마나 걸려요?
기사: 지금은 길이 막힐 테니까 한 시간쯤
        걸릴 거예요.

<정답>
리리: 인사동
비비엔: 교보문고

Lesson 6: Practice 2. Online audio file 06:05

듣기 연습 2
1) 퍼디
저기: 저기 보이는 사거리에서 좌회전할까요?
퍼디: 네, 좌회전해서 50미터쯤 가면 주유소가
      보일 테니까 그 앞에 세워 주세요.
저기: 네, 알겠습니다.

2) 벤슨
기사: 손님, 어디에 세울까요?
벤슨: 횡단보도 앞에 세워 주세요.
기사: 네, 알겠습니다.

<정답>
퍼 디: 주유소 앞
벤 슨: 횡단보도 앞

Lesson 7: online audio file 05:26

준 이 치: 스테파니 씨, 지난 주말에 뭐 했어요?
스테파니: 등산을 했는데 단풍이 아주 예뻤어요.
　　　　　준이치 씨는 지난 주말에 뭐 했어요?
준 이 치: 저는 농구를 했는데 아주 재미있었어요.
　　　　　스테파니 씨, 내일은 뭐 할 거예요?
스테파니: 내일은 약속이 없어요.
준 이 치: 그럼, 대학로에서 뮤지컬을 하는데
　　　　　같이 볼까요?
스테파니: 네, 좋아요. 같이 봅시다.

<정답>
문제 1: 1) 농구　2) 등산
문제 2: 뮤지컬 보기

Lesson 8: Practice 1. Online audio file 07:55

듣기 연습 1
1) 최지영
의사:　　어디가 아프세요?
최지영:　저는 배가 아프고 식욕이 없어요.

2) 요나단
의사:　　어디가 아프세요?
요나단:　저는 눈이 아프고 눈물이 나요.

3) 비비엔
의 사:　　어디가 아프세요?
비비엔:　저는 기침이 나고 콧물이 나요.

4) 벤슨
의사:　　어디가 아프세요?
벤슨:　　저는 메스껍고 설사를 해요.

<정답>
1) 최지영: (②, ⑦)
최지영 씨는 배가 아프고 식욕이 없어요.
2) 요나단: (④, ⑭)
요나단 씨는 눈이 아프고 눈물이 나요.
3) 비비엔 : (⑨, ⑩)
비비엔 씨는 기침이 나고 콧물이 나요.
4) 벤슨 : (⑧, ⑫)
벤슨 씨는 메스껍고 설사를 해요.

Lesson 8: Practice 2. Online audio file 09:34

듣기 연습 2
안녕하세요? 민속박물관 관람 안내입니다.
우리 박물관 전시실에서는 사진을 찍으면 안 되고
담배를 피우면 안 됩니다. 작품을 손으로 만지면
안 됩니다. 그리고 큰 소리로 떠들면 안 되고
박물관 안에서 뛰면 안 됩니다. 휴게실에서는
간단한 식사를 해도 되고 커피를 마셔도 됩니다.
그럼 즐거운 시간 보내세요.

<정답>
문제 1: ①, ④, ⑤, ⑨, ⑩
문제 2: ②, ⑦, ⑧

Lesson 9: online audio file 04:39

앙리: 하즈키 씨, 이번 주말에 뭐 할 거예요?
하즈키: 저는 수영하러 바다에 갈 거예요.
앙리: 우아! 하즈키 씨 수영을 잘하세요?
하즈키: 아니요, 조금 해요.
앙리: 앙리 씨도 수영을 좋아하세요?
저도 아주 좋아해요.
고등학교 때 수영 선수였어요.
하즈키: 우아! 그럼 이번 주말에 우리 같이
수영하러 갈까요?
앙리: 미안하지만, 이번 주말에는 못 가요.
하즈키: 왜요?
앙리: 약속이 있어서 못 가요.
하즈키: 그럼 다음 주말에 같이 갑시다.
앙리: 네, 좋아요.

<정답>
문제 1: 수영
문제 2: 앙리가 약속이 있어서
문제 3: 다음 주말

Lesson 10: Practice 1. Online audio file 05:35

듣기 연습 1
이 사람들은 모두 제 친구들이에요.
친구들은 이번 주말에 아주 바빠요.
스테파니 씨는 스키를 타러 평창에 가요.
스테파니 씨는 스키를 아주 잘 타요.
그리고 열심히 태권도를 하는 사람은 벤슨 씨예요.
벤슨 씨는 다음 달에 태권도 시합이 있어서
요즘 바빠요. 영화를 보러 영화관에 가는 사람은
리리 씨와 이준기 씨예요.
그리고 음악을 듣고 있는 사람은 비비엔 씨예요.
요리를 하고 있는 사람은 하즈키 씨예요.
하즈키 씨는 요리를 아주 좋아해요.
커피를 마시고 있는 사람은 아마니 씨와 퍼디 씨
예요.

<정답>
① 벤슨 ② 비비엔 ③ 스테파니
④ 아마니, 퍼디 ⑤ 이준기, 리리

Lesson 10: Practice 2. Online audio file 07:31

듣기 연습 2

오늘은 비비엔 씨의 생일이에요. 그래서 친구들과
같이 비비엔 씨의 집에서 생일 파티를 했어요.
스테파니 씨는 파란 원피스를 입고 노란 가방을 들고
있어요. 그리고 줄무늬 양복을 입고 있는 사람은
벤슨 씨예요. 꽃무늬 블라우스를 입고 벤슨 씨와
이야기하고 있는 사람은 비비엔 씨예요. 청바지와
하얀 티셔츠를 입고 있는 사람은 이준기 씨예요.
그리고 까만 안경을 쓰고 물방울무늬 넥타이를
매고 있는 사람은 퍼디 씨예요. 빨간 모자를 쓰고
커피를 마시고 있는 사람은 아마니 씨예요.
생일 파티는 아주 재미있었어요.

<정답>
① 비비엔 ② 벤슨 ③ 퍼디 ④ 이준기 ⑤ 스테파니

Lesson 11: online audio file 05:29

지금 이 도시는 아주 복잡합니다.
그렇지만 10년 전에는 복잡하지 않았습니다.
10년 전과 비교하면 이 도시는 아주 복잡해졌습니다.
자동차도 10년 전보다 많아졌어요. 그래서 길도
넓어졌어요. 그리고 높은 빌딩도 많이 생겼어요.
10년 전에는 약국이 있었지만 지금은 없어지고
병원이 생겼어요. 작은 가게가 없어지고
대형 마트가 생겼어요. 작은 식당이 없어지고
빌딩 3층에 큰 레스토랑이 생겼어요.
거리에 사람들도 많아졌어요.
사람들이 휴대폰을 사용해서 공중전화도 없어졌어요.
하지만 우체국은 그대로 있어요.

<정답>
그림 1

Lesson 12: online audio file 05:14

앙리: 비비엔 씨, 이번 방학에 고향에 갈 거예요?
비비엔: 아니요, 저는 안 갈 거예요.
앙리: 그럼 비비엔 씨, 여행을 좋아하세요?
비비엔: 네, 좋아해요.
앙리: 그럼, 우리 같이 제주도에 갈까요?
비비엔: 좋아요. 제주도에서 한라산에 올라갈까요?
앙리: 미안하지만, 다리가 아파서 등산은 못 해요.
비비엔: 그래요!
앙리: 그럼, 바다에서 수영할까요?
비비엔: 저는 수영을 못 해요.
앙리: 그럼, 번지점프를 할 수 있어요?
비비엔: 네, 하고 싶어요.
앙리: 좋아요. 그리고 맛있는 생선회를 먹을까요?
비비엔: 저는 알러지가 있어서 생선회를 먹을 수
         없어요.
앙리: 그럼, 돼지고기는 먹을 수 있어요?
비비엔: 네, 먹을 수 있어요. 삼겹살을 아주
         좋아해요.

<정답>
문제 1: ③, ⑧
문제 2: ④, ⑤, ⑩

Translation of Talking with Lee Joon-gi

Lesson 1, page 29

Lee Joon-gi

Hello! This is a photo of my family.
There are five people in my family altogether.
There's my grandfather, father and mother.
Also, I have one younger sister.
My grandfather is a postman.
My father is a doctor. He works at a hospital.
My mother is a cook. She works at a restaurant.
My younger sister is a high school student. She goes to Hanguk High School.
And me, I'm a movie actor.

Hazuki

Hello! This is a photo of my family.
There are three people in my family altogether.
There's my father, mother and me.
My father is a postman. He works at the post office.
My mother is a teacher. She works at a school.
And me, I'm a university student. I go to Hanguk University.

Lesson 2, page 45

Joon-gi: Vivien, do you have any Korean friends?
Viven: No, I don't.
Joon-gi: What kind of people do you like?
Viven: I like tall, kind people.
Joon-gi: Oh, really? In that case, would you like me to introduce you to my friend?
Viven: Yes, I would. What kind of person is he?
Joon-gi: My friend is smart, quiet and kind.
Viven: OK, great. I like smart people. So when will we meet?
Joon-gi: Let's meet in Myeongdong this weekend.
Viven: Alright.

Lesson 3, page 61

Lee Joon-gi

Hello everyone! This is Lee Joon-gi.
Right now, I'm shooting a film in Sydney.
When the filming is over, I'm going to go to the zoo and see a koala.
And tomorrow, I'm going to meet Stephanie.
When class is over, Stephanie is going to come to the place where I'm filming.
We are going to go to the beach together.
At the beach, we are both going to swim and have a delicious dinner.
Have a fun vacation, everybody.

Vivien

Hello everyone! This is Vivien.
Right now, I'm studying drawing in Paris.
When class is over today, I'm going to go with my friends to the Eiffel Tower.
We are going to drink coffee and take pictures at the Eiffel Tower.
When I finish studying drawing in Paris, I'm going to go to Korea.
I'm going to become a designer in Korea.
See you in Korea.

Lesson 4, page 81

Joon-gi: Amani, how have you been doing lately?

Amani: Lately, I have been studying for the TOPIK.

Joon-gi: Oh, really? So the test is next week?

Amani: Yeah. That's why I've been so busy lately.

Joon-gi: What do you want to do when you graduate?

Amani: I want to go to Saudi Arabia and become a news anchor.

Joon-gi: Ah, I see.

Amani: What do you want to do when you graduate?

Joon-gi: I want to marry my pretty girlfriend.

Amani: Wow! Do you have a girlfriend?

Joon-gi: No, I don't have one yet. If you know someone good, please introduce her.

Lesson 5, page 99

Hazuki: Excuse me, where is the hospital?

Joon-gi: Go straight on this road and turn left at the second traffic light.

Hazuki: Will I see it as soon as I turn left at the second traffic light?

Joon-gi: If you turn left and go straight, there will be a bank. Go straight on the road next to the bank, and you will see the Happiness Building. The hospital is on the third floor of the Happiness Building.

Hazuki: How long will it take to walk from here?

Joon-gi: It takes around fifteen minutes on foot.

Hazuki: OK. Thanks.

Lesson 6, page 115

Taxi Driver: Please get in. Where would you like to go, sir?

Joon-gi: Please take me to Yeouido.

Taxi Driver: Alright.

Joon-gi: How long does it take to get to Yeouido from here?

Taxi Driver: If traffic is bad, it takes around an hour. Traffic shouldn't be very bad at this time of day, so we will probably get there in forty minutes.

Joon-gi: Alright.

Taxi Driver: Good grief! Everyone's going home from work, so there's a lot of traffic.

Joon-gi: Is there no faster way?

Taxi Driver: There is a detour we could take. It will probably be faster than this route.

Joon-gi: Then let's take the fast route.

Taxi Driver: OK. Should we turn right at the four-way intersection over there?

Joon-gi: Yes. As soon as you turn right you will see a crosswalk. Please stop in front of that.

Taxi Driver: Alright. Where do you want me to stop?

Joon-gi: Please stop in front of the white building over there. How much is it?

Taxi Driver: It's 13,000 won.

Joon-gi: Here you are. Thanks.

Taxi Driver: Thank you. Goodbye.

Lesson 7, page 137

Stephanie: Hello. Is this Lee Joon-gi's house?

Joon-gi's mother: Yes, it is. May I ask who is speaking?

Stephanie: It's Stephanie, Joon-gi's friend. Is Joon-gi there?

Joon-gi's mother: Ah, Stephanie. It's been a while. Please wait a moment.

Joon-gi: Hi, Stephanie. It's me.

Stephanie: Joon-gi, what did you do last weekend?

Joon-gi: I was on a film shoot in Beijing. I had a really hard time.

Stephanie: I went with my friends to the beach. It was very beautiful.

Joon-gi: Oh, I see! By the way, Stephanie, why are you calling?

Stephanie: Joon-gi, tomorrow is my day off. What are you going to do?

Joon-gi: There is going to be a press screening for a movie, would you like to go together?

Stephanie: Sure, that sounds great. Let's go together. I'll call you tomorrow.

Lesson 8, page 160

Doctor: What's the matter?

Joon-gi: Since yesterday, my eyes have been hurting and watery.

Doctor: Let me take a look. OK, you have an eye infection that has been going around lately.

Joon-gi: I have a movie to shoot this afternoon. Can I go to the film set?

Doctor: You can't go out. Rest at home for about three days. Here's your prescription. Go to a pharmacy to get your medicine.

Joon-gi: Alright. Thank you.

At the Pharmacy

Pharmacist: Lee Joon-gi, here are your eye drops. Put them in your eyes once every two hours.

Joon-gi: Alright, thanks.

Lesson 9, pages 177–179

Talking with Lee Joon-gi 1

Joon-gi: Lili, what are you doing this weekend? Let's see . . . I don't have any plans yet. What about you?

Joon-gi: I'm going to head to Pyeongchang to go skiing.

Lili: Wow! Are you good at skiing?

Joon-gi: Not really. I'm OK at skiing. Do you like skiing, too?

Lili: Yes, I do.

Joon-gi: Well, why don't you come this weekend too?

Lili: I'm sorry, but I can't go this weekend.

Joon-gi: Why not?

Lili: My leg hurts, so I can't go skiing.

Joon-gi: Come with us next weekend, then.

Lili: OK, great.

Talking with Lee Joon-gi 2

Joon-gi

My name is Lee Joon-gi, and I'm Korean.

Lately, I have been shooting a film.

I really like Bulgogi.

Bulgogi is expensive, but I like it because it tastes good.

I like spring because it's warm.

I like apples because they taste good.

Also, I like taekwondo because it's good for your health.

Lately, though, I've been busy, so I haven't been able to practice very often.

This weekend, I'm going to go to the dojang to practice taekwondo.

I'm also going to go to Busan to see my friends.

I'm going to eat sashimi with my friends.

Vivien

My name is Vivien. I'm German.

I'm studying Korean at Hanguk University and teaching skiing at DK Ski Resort.

I really like Bibimbap. Bibimbap is spicy, but I like it because there are a lot of vegetables in it.

I like winter because it snows, and I like bananas because they are easy to eat.

I really like swimming because it helps with dieting. Lately, though, I've been busy so I haven't been able to go very often.

This weekend, I'm going to go to the swimming pool to go swimming.

I'm also going to go to Myeongdong to meet my friends. In Myeongdong, I'm going to watch a scary movie with my friends.

Lesson 10, page 197

Hazuki: Who are all these people?

Joon-gi: They are all my friends.

Hazuki: Wow! Who is the person wearing the flower-print dress?

Joon-gi: That's Stephanie.

Hazuki: Who is the person wearing jeans and a red T-shirt?

Joon-gi: That's Vivien. The jeans look great on her, don't they?

Hazuki: Yes. Who is the person in the black suit?

Joon-gi: The person wearing the glasses? That's Junichi.

Hazuki: Ah! So where are you?

Joon-gi: I'm the person next to Stephanie wearing the yellow T-shirt.

Hazuki: Wow! You really look great!

Lesson 11, page 216

Joon-gi

Hello everyone. This is Lee Joon-gi. This is my hometown.

Right now, my hometown is very crowded. But ten years ago, it wasn't crowded.

Compared with ten years ago, it has gotten more crowded.

There are more cars now than ten years ago.

That's why the roads have gotten wider.

Also, a lot of tall buildings have been built.

Ten years ago, there was a pharmacy, but now that is gone and a hospital has taken its place.

Small stores have disappeared and a supermarket has come in.

A big restaurant moved into the third story of a building.

When I was young, I played basketball with my friends in the vacant lot in front of our village.

But now, a gymnasium has moved into that vacant lot.

There are also more people on the street.

Since everyone uses mobile phones, the payphones have vanished as well.

However, the post office and the gimbap diner are still there.

Lesson 12, pages 233–234

Joon-gi

Hello everyone. This is Lee Joon-gi.

Today, I was invisible all day long.

I went to the film studio in the morning without taking a shower.

I could see the other actors and staff, but they couldn't see me.

So during the break time, I secretly carried the camera for the cinematographer and massaged his shoulders.

The cinematographer was surprised, but he probably felt better.

In the afternoon, I got on a plane for free and went to Sydney.

It's winter in Korea, but right now it's summer in Sydney, so I went swimming in the ocean.

Today I could do whatever I wanted, so I was very happy.

Vivien

Hello everyone! This is Vivien.

Today, I was invisible all day long.

In the morning, I went to school.

I could see the teacher and my friends, but they couldn't see me.

That is why I secretly ate Lili's bread and Ferdy's banana.

Lili and Ferdy were surprised when their bread and banana disappeared.

Then I drank Roy's coffee. Roy was also surprised when his coffee vanished.

Then, when class was over, I secretly carried my teacher's bag.

My teacher said, "Huh, my bag is light today."

My teacher probably felt good.

So I was in a good mood today.

Answers to the Exercises

Lesson 1

Page 23

학교랑 도서관
선생님이랑 학생

외할머니께서/외할머니께서는
삼촌께서/삼촌께서는
고모께서/고모께서는

Page 24

나 다섯 명
가 퍼디 씨, 가족이 몇 명이에요?
나 우리 가족은 모두 여섯 명이에요.
가 비비엔 씨, 가족이 몇 명이에요?
나 우리 가족은 모두 열 두 명이에요.

Page 25

나 두 명
가 어서 오세요. 모두 몇 분이세요?
나 모두 다섯 명이에요.
가 어서 오세요. 모두 몇 분이세요?
나 모두 일곱 명이에요.

Page 26

가 스테파니 씨, 이 사람들은 누구예요?
나 하즈키 씨랑 요나단 씨예요.
가 스테파니 씨, 이것은 뭐예요?
나 컴퓨터랑 책이에요.

Page 27

가 어머니께서는 무엇을 하세요?
나 어머니는 요리사예요. 레스토랑에서 일하세요.
가 누나는 뭐 해요?
나 누나는 스튜어디스예요. 호주항공에서 일해요.

Lesson 2

Page 39

차가운 녹차
단 초콜릿
힘든 운동
재미있는 영화
착한 여자 친구
작은 가방
시끄러운 장소

밝은 방
예쁜 여자
많은 사람
친절한 선생님
무뚝뚝한 남자 친구
추운 날씨
맑은 눈

Pages 40~41

가 운동을
나 배구를
가 리리 씨, 무슨 과일을 좋아하세요?
나 저는 파인애플을 좋아해요.
가 리리 씨, 무슨 과일을 좋아하세요?
나 저는 포도를 좋아해요.
가 리리 씨, 무슨 음식을 좋아하세요?
나 저는 김밥을 좋아해요.
가 리리 씨, 무슨 음식을 좋아하세요?
나 저는 돈가스를 좋아해요.

Page 42

가 사과는, 과일
나 사과는 단
가 수영은 어떤 운동이에요?
나 수영은 힘든 운동이에요.
가 떡볶이는 어떤 음식이에요?
나 떡볶이는 매운 음식이에요.

Page 43
가 어떤 사람이에요?
나 머리가 좋고 재미있는
가 어떤 사람이에요?
나 키가 작고 귀여운 사람이에요.
가 어떤 사람이에요?
나 똑똑하고 키가 큰 사람이에요.

Lesson 3

Page 53
시험이 끝나면
친구를 만나면
케이크를 만들면
소문을 들으면
기분이 나쁘면
일이 끝나면
일등을 하면
침대에 누우면

돈이 많으면
시간이 있으면
날씨가 더우면
기분이 좋으면
졸리면
학교에 가면
무서우면
집이 멀면

Page 55
사진을 찍을 거예요.
그림을 그릴 거예요.
쉴 거예요.
영화를 볼 거예요.
비빔밥을 먹을 거예요.
책을 읽을 거예요.
친구를 만날 거예요.
이메일을 보낼 거예요.

음악을 들을 거예요.
김치를 담글 거예요.
휴지를 주울 거예요.
가야금을 배울 거예요.
설거지를 할 거예요.
산책을 할 거예요.
책상을 정리할 거예요.
잠을 잘 거예요.

Pages 56–57
가 비비엔, 시간이 있으면
나 시간이 있으면
가 비비엔 씨, 한국말을 잘하면 뭐 해요?
나 한국말을 잘하면 한국어 선생님이 돼요.
가 비비엔 씨, 수업이 끝나면 뭐 해요?
나 수업이 끝나면 콘서트에 가요
가 비비엔 씨, 숙제를 다 하면 뭐 해요?
나 숙제를 다 하면 음악을 들어요.
가 비비엔 씨, 바다에 가면 뭐 해요?
나 바다에 가면 수영해요.

Page 58–59
가 리리, 내일 뭐 할 거예요?
나 내일 친구를 만날 거예요.
가 리리 씨, 내일 뭐 할 거예요?
나 저는 내일 번지점프를 할 거예요.
가 리리 씨, 내일 뭐 할 거예요?
나 저는 내일 야구장에 갈 거예요.
가 리리 씨, 주말에 뭐 할 거예요?
나 저는 주말에 슈퍼에 갈 거예요.
가 리리 씨, 주말에 뭐 할 거예요?
나 저는 주말에 김치를 담글 거예요.

Lesson 4

Page 73

영화를 보고 싶다./영화를 보고 싶어 하다.
이준기를 만나고 싶다./이준기를 만나고 싶어 하다.
떡볶이를 먹고 싶다./떡볶이를 먹고 싶어 하다.
녹차를 마시고 싶다./녹차를 마시고 싶어 하다.
결혼을 하고 싶다./결혼을 하고 싶어 하다.
가수가 되고 싶다./가수가 되고 싶어 하다.
스키를 타고 싶다./스키를 타고 싶어 하다.
태권도를 배우고 싶다./태권도를 배우고 싶어 하다.
사인을 받고 싶다./사인을 받고 싶어 하다.
선물을 준비하고 싶다./선물을 준비하고 싶어 하다.
휴대폰을 사고 싶다./휴대폰을 사고 싶어 하다.
여자 친구를 사귀고 싶다./여자 친구를 사귀고
싶어 하다.
삼성에 취업하고 싶다./삼성에 취업하고 싶어 하다.

Page 74

가 케이크예요.
나 이것이 케이크군요!
가 이것은 떡이에요.
나 아! 이것이 떡이군요!
가 이것은 떡볶이예요.
나 아! 이것이 떡볶이군요!

Page 75

가 지금 뭐 해요?
나 농구를 해요.
가 농구를 하는군요!
가 지금 뭐 해요?
나 저는 지금 김치를 담가요.
가 아! 김치를 담그는군요.

Pages 76–77

가 졸업을 하면 뭐 할 거예요?
나 졸업을 하면 경찰관이 될 거예요.

가 졸업을 하면 뭐 할 거예요?
나 저는 졸업을 하면 통역관이 될 거예요.
가 졸업을 하면 뭐 할 거예요?
나 저는 졸업을 하면 아나운서가 될 거예요.
가 졸업을 하면 뭐 할 거예요?
나 저는 졸업을 하면 요리사가 될 거예요.
가 졸업을 하면 뭐 할 거예요?
나 저는 졸업을 하면 한국어 선생님이 될 거예요.

Pages 78–79

가 뭐 하고 싶어요?
나 커피를 마시고 싶어요.
가 커피를 마시고 싶어 해요.
가 뭐 하고 싶어요?
나 저는 요리를 하고 싶어요.
가 퍼디 씨는 요리를 하고 싶어 해요.
가 뭐 하고 싶어요?
나 저는 드럼을 치고 싶어요.
가 이준기 씨는 드럼을 치고 싶어 해요.
가 뭐 하고 싶어요?
나 저는 콘서트에 가고 싶어요.
가 하즈키 씨는 콘서트에 가고 싶어 해요.

Lesson 5

Page 89

밥을 먹다가 전화를 했어요.
남자 친구와 싸우다가 울었어요.
책을 읽다가 잤어요.
숙제를 하다가 편지를 썼어요.
술을 마시다가 노래를 했어요.
영화를 보다가 친구를 생각했어요.
도서관에 가다가 커피를 샀어요.
잠을 자다가 놀라서 깼어요.

Page 92

가 사무실이 어디예요?
나 사무실은 왼쪽으로 가세요.

가 실례지만, 광화문이 어디예요?
나 광화문은 저쪽으로 가세요.
가 실례지만, 우체국이 어디예요?
나 우체국은 옆으로 가세요.

Page 93

가 한국에서 일본까지 얼마나 걸려요?
나 일본까지 비행기로 두 시간쯤 걸려요.
가 한국에서 스페인까지 얼마나 걸려요?
나 스페인까지 배로 두 달쯤 걸려요.
가 집에서 명동까지 얼마나 걸려요?
나 명동까지 걸어서 20분쯤 걸려요.

Pages 94–95

가 도서관
나 오른쪽으로 가다가 사거리에서 왼쪽으로 가세요.
가 실례지만, 은행이 어디예요?
나 옆길로 가다가 육교를 건너세요.
가 실례지만, 백화점이 어디예요?
나 사거리에서 왼쪽으로 가다가
　　아래로 50m쯤 가세요.
가 실례지만, 우체국이 어디예요?
나 은행 옆길로 가다가 육교를 건너세요.
가 실례지만, 한국대학교가 어디예요?
나 뒤로 돌아서 100m쯤 가다가 왼쪽으로 가세요.
가 실례지만, 국회의사당이 어디예요?
나 이쪽으로 쭉 가다가 오른쪽으로 가세요.

Pages 96–97

가 어제 뭐 했어요?
나 요리하다가 설거지를 했어요.
가 어제 뭐 했어요?
나 영화를 보다가 울었어요.
가 어제 뭐 했어요?
나 숙제를 하다가 잠을 잤어요.
가 어제 뭐 했어요?
나 청소하다가 전화를 했어요.
가 어제 뭐 했어요?
나 음악을 듣다가 잤어요.
가 어제 뭐 했어요?
나 술을 마시다가 노래했어요.

Lesson 6

Page 108

열어 주세요.
닫아 주세요.
만들어 주세요.
출발해 주세요.
들어 주세요.
입어 주세요.
더울 테니까
바쁠 테니까
청소할 테니까
차가 막힐 테니까
앉을 테니까
멀 테니까

Page 110

가 어디로 갈까요?
나 한국대학교로 가 주세요.
가 손님, 어디로 갈까요?
나 우리병원으로 가 주세요.
가 손님, 어디로 갈까요?
나 교보문고로 가 주세요.

Page 111

가 어디에 세워 드릴까요?
나 지하철역 근처에 세워 주세요.
가 손님, 어디에 세워 드릴까요?
나 주유소 앞에 세워 주세요.
가 손님, 어디에 세워 드릴까요?
나 횡단보도 근처에 세워 주세요.

Pages 112–113

깎아 줄 테니까 또 오세요.
내일 추울 테니까 따뜻하게 입으세요.
케이크를 만들 테니까 선물을 사 오세요.
도와줄 테니까 걱정하지 마세요.
우산을 빌려줄 테니까 걱정하지 마세요.
빌려줄 테니까 사지 마세요.

Lesson 7

Page 125
친구지요?/친구였지요?
선배지요?/선배였지요?
학생이지요?/학생이었지요?
선생님이지요?/선생님이었지요?
아프지요?/아팠지요?
많지요?/많았지요?
괜찮지요?/괜찮았지요?
쓸쓸하지요?/쓸쓸했지요?
힘들지요?/힘들었지요?
괴롭지요?/괴로웠지요?

Page 127
학교인데/학교였는데
휴일인데/휴일이었는데
주말인데/주말이었는데
시험인데/시험이었는데

Page 129
친구를 기다리는데/친구를 기다렸는데
커피를 마시는데/커피를 마셨는데
농구를 하는데/농구를 했는데
침대에 눕는데/침대에 누웠는데
꿈을 꾸는데/꿈을 꿨는데
학교가 먼데/학교가 멀었는데
날씨가 더운데/날씨가 더웠는데
영화가 재미있는데/영화가 재미있었는데
돈이 없는데/돈이 없었는데
조용한데/조용했는데

Pages 130–131
가 퍼디 씨의 아버지지요?
나 네, 맞아요.
가 내일 시험이지요?
나 아니요, 수업이에요.
가 떡볶이가 맵지요?
나 네, 맞아요.
가 커피를 마시지요?
나 아니요, 차를 마셔요.

Page 132
가 내일은 휴일인데 뮤지컬을 보러 갈까요?
나 네, 좋아요. 뮤지컬을 보러 갑시다.
가 스테파니 씨, 오늘은 리리 씨의 생일인데
가 파티할까요?
나 네, 좋아요. 파티합시다.
가 스테파니 씨, 다음 주는 시험인데 같이
  공부할까요?
나 네 좋아요. 같이 공부합시다.

Pages 133–134
가 이번 주말에 여의도에 가는데 같이 갈까요?
나 같이 갑시다.
가 스테파니 씨, 내일 박물관에 가는데 같이
  갈까요?
나 네, 좋아요. 같이 갑시다.
가 스테파니 씨, 오늘 바쁜데 내일 만날까요?
나 네, 좋아요. 내일 만납시다.
가 스테파니 씨, 내일 수업이 없는데 농구를
  할까요?
나 네, 좋아요. 농구를 합시다.

Pages 134–135
가 지난 주말에 뭐 하셨어요?
나 저는 지난 주말에 롯데월드에 갔는데
  아주 즐거웠어요.
가 어제 뭐 하셨어요?
나 저는 어제 영화를 봤는데 너무 슬펐어요.
가 어제 뭐 하셨어요?
나 저는 어제 불고기를 먹었는데 아주 맛있었어요.

Lesson 8

Page 149
커피를 마셔도 돼요?
술을 마셔도 돼요?
돼지고기를 먹어도 돼요?
담배를 피워도 돼요? 일해도 돼요? 수영해도 돼요?
사진을 찍어도 돼요?
잠을 자도 돼요?

만져도 돼요?
복도에서 뛰어도 돼요?
샤워를 해도 돼요?
떠들어도 돼요?
앉아도 돼요?
누워도 돼요?
구워도 돼요? 걸어도 돼요? 닫아도 돼요?

Page 151
커피를 마시면 안 돼요.
술을 마시면 안 돼요.
돼지고기를 먹으면 안 돼요.
테니스를 치면 안 돼요.
담배를 피우면 안 돼요.
일하면 안 돼요.
수영하면 안 돼요.
사진을 찍으면 안 돼요.
잠을 자면 안 돼요.
만지면 안 돼요.
샤워를 하면 안 돼요.
떠들면 안 돼요.
앉으면 안 돼요.
누우면 안 돼요.
구우면 안 돼요.
걸으면 안 돼요.
닫으면 안 돼요.

Pages 152–153
가 아프세요?
나 머리가 아프고 열이 나요.
가 어디가 아프세요?
나 저는 재채기가 나고 콧물이 나요.
가 어디가 아프세요?
나 저는 메스껍고 토해요.
가 어디가 아프세요?
나 저는 배가 아프고 설사를 해요.
가 어디가 아프세요?
나 저는 기침이 나고 오한이 나요
가 어디가 아프세요?
나 저는 눈물이 나고 눈이 아파요.
가 어디가 아프세요?
나 저는 이가 아프고 피가 나요.

Pages 154–155
가 담배를 피워도 돼요?
나 담배를 피워도 돼요.
가 리리 씨, 아이스크림을 먹어도 돼요?
나 네, 아이스크림을 먹어도 돼요.
가 리리 씨, 샤워해도 돼요?
나 네, 샤워해도 돼요.
가 리리 씨, 술을 마셔도 돼요?
나 네, 술을 마셔도 돼요.
가 리리 씨, 수영해도 돼요?
나 네, 수영해도 돼요.

Pages 156–157
가 아이스크림을 먹어도 돼요?
나 아이스크림을 먹으면 안 돼요.
가 앙리 씨, 샤워해도 돼요?
나 아니요, 샤워하면 안 돼요.
가 앙리 씨, 돼지고기를 먹어도 돼요?
나 아니요, 돼지고기를 먹으면 안 돼요.
가 앙리 씨, TV를 봐도 돼요?
나 아니요, TV를 보면 안 돼요.
가 앙리 씨, 술을 마셔도 돼요?
나 아니요, 술을 마시면 안 돼요.

Lesson 9

Page 169
번지점프를 하러 가요.
삼계탕을 먹으러 가요.
수영하러 가요.
김치를 담그러 가요.
옷을 사러 가요.
잠을 자러 가요.

음악을 들으러 가요.
맥주를 마시러 가요
친구를 도우러 가요.
태권도를 배우러 가요.
책을 읽으러 가요.
공연을 보러 가요.
쇼핑하러 가요.

Page 171

감기에 걸려서
늦잠을 자서
길이 막혀서
매워서
짧아서
주워서
길어서
걸어서
조용해서

Pages 172–173

가 어제 왜 축구를 안 했어요?
나 저는 어제 다리가 아파서 축구를 못 했어요.
가 오늘 왜 영화를 안 봤어요?
나 저는 오늘 숙제가 많아서 영화를 못 봤어요.
가 주말에 왜 롯데월드에 안 갔어요?
나 저는 주말에 바빠서 롯데월드에 못 갔어요.
가 어제 왜 수영을 안 했어요?
나 저는 어제 감기에 걸려서 수영을 못 했어요.
가 오늘 왜 밥을 안 먹었어요?
나 저는 오늘 배가 아파서 밥을 못 먹었어요.

Pages 174–175

가 어디에 가세요?
나 커피를 마시러 카페에 가요.
가 하즈키 씨, 어디에 가세요?
나 저는 검도하러 검도장에 가요.
가 하즈키 씨, 어디에 가세요?
나 저는 불고기를 먹으러 식당에 가요.
가 하즈키 씨, 어디에 가세요?
나 저는 스키를 타러 스키장에 가요.
가 하즈키 씨, 어디에 가세요?
나 저는 태권도를 하러 태권도장에 가요.

Lesson 10

Page 187

원피스를 입고 있다.
모자를 쓰고 있다.
구두를 신고 있다.

양말을 신고 있다.
넥타이를 매고 있다.
팔찌를 하고 있다.
장갑을 끼고 있다.
목걸이를 하고 있다.
안경을 쓰고 있다.
가방을 들고 있다.

Page 189

잠을 자는 시간
마시는 커피
좋아하는 운동
못 먹는 음식
일어나는 시간
부산에 가는 버스
호떡을 파는 사람

Pages 190–191

가 누구예요?
나 스테파니 씨는 파란 구두를 신고 있어요.
가 누구예요?
나 아마니 씨는 장갑을 끼고 있어요.
가 누구예요?
나 벤슨 씨는 줄무늬 셔츠를 입고 있어요.
가 누구예요?
나 준이치 씨는 큰 가방을 메고 있어요.
가 누구예요?
나 하즈키 씨는 빨간 모자를 쓰고 있어요.

Page 192–193

가 마시는
나 스테파니 씨가 마시는 커피는 카푸치노예요.
가 부르는 노래가 뭐예요?
나 벤슨 씨가 부르는 노래는 한국 노래예요.
가 기다리는 버스가 뭐예요?
나 하즈키 씨가 기다리는 버스는 8000번이에요.
가 보는 드라마가 뭐예요?
나 비비엔 씨가 보는 드라마는 <아랑사또전>이에요.
가 듣는 음악이 뭐예요?
나 앙리 씨가 듣는 음악은 K-POP이에요.
가 좋아하는 운동이 뭐예요?
나 아마니 씨가 좋아하는 운동은 골프예요.

Pages 194–195

가 마시는

나 스테파니 씨가 마시는 커피는 뜨거워요.

가 보는 영화는 어때요?

나 비비엔 씨가 보는 영화는 슬퍼요.

가 다니는 학교는 어때요?

나 아마니 씨가 다니는 학교는 멀어요.

가 만나는 친구는 어때요?

나 요나단 씨가 만나는 친구는 예뻐요.

가 읽는 책은 어때요?

나 앙리 씨가 읽는 책은 어려워요.

가 먹는 김치찌개는 어때요?

나 퍼디 씨가 먹는 김치찌개는 매워요.

Lesson 11

Page 205

좋아졌어요.

키가 커졌어요.

날씬해졌어요.

따뜻해졌어요.

작아졌어요.

적어졌어요.

나빠졌어요.

길어졌어요.

뚱뚱해졌어요.

추워졌어요.

바빠졌어요.

아름다워졌어요.

Page 207

길거리보다 소극장

주점보다 북카페

Page 209

영화를 볼 때/영화를 봤을 때

친구를 만날 때/친구를 만났을 때

기분이 나쁠 때/기분이 나빴을 때

시간이 많을 때/시간이 많았을 때

돈이 없을 때/돈이 없었을 때

고등학교에 다닐 때/고등학교에 다녔을 때

피자를 먹을 때/피자를 먹었을 때

여자 친구와 헤어질 때/여자 친구와 헤어졌을 때

남자 친구와 싸울 때/남자 친구와 싸웠을 때

수업을 할 때/수업을 했을 때

떡볶이가 매울 때/떡볶이가 매웠을 때

길을 걸을 때/길을 걸었을 때

꽃을 팔 때/꽃을 팔았을 때

Pages 210–211

가 요즘 날씨가

나 요즘 날씨가 지난주보다 추워졌어요.

가 한국의 교통이 어때요?

나 한국의 교통이 5년 전보다 복잡해졌어요.

가 한국어 공부가 어때요?

나 한국어 공부가 초급보다 어려워졌어요.

가 지금 기분이 어때요?

나 지금 기분이 밤보다 좋아졌어요.

가 요즘 하즈키 씨가 어때요?

나 요즘 하즈키 씨가 한 달 전보다 날씬해졌어요.

Page 212

가 영화를 볼 때 보통 뭐 해요?

나 저는 영화를 볼 때 보통 팝콘을 먹어요.

가 피곤할 때 보통 뭐 해요?

나 저는 피곤할 때 보통 샤워해요.

가 기분이 좋을 때 보통 뭐 해요?

나 저는 기분이 좋을 때 보통 친구를 만나요.

Page 213

가 술을 마셨을 때 보통 뭐 했어요?

나 저는 술을 마셨을 때 보통 노래를 했어요.

가 기분이 나빴을 때 보통 뭐 했어요?

나 저는 기분이 나빴을 때 보통 맛있는 음식을
먹었어요.

가 친구를 만났을 때 보통 뭐 했어요?

나 저는 친구를 만났을 때 보통 영화를 봤어요.

Lesson 12

Page 225
번지점프를 할 수 있어요./번지점프를 할 수 없어요.
삼계탕을 먹을 수 있어요./삼계탕을 먹을 수 없어요.
소주를 마실 수 있어요./소주를 마실 수 없어요.
기숙사에 살 수 있어요./기숙사에 살 수 없어요.
태권도를 할 수 있어요./태권도를 할 수 없어요.

Page 227
번지점프를 못 해요./번지점프를 안 해요.
삼계탕을 못 먹어요./삼계탕을 안 먹어요.
케이크를 못 만들어요./케이크를 안 만들어요.
매운 음식을 못 먹어요./매운 음식을 안 먹어요.
피아노를 못 쳐요./피아노를 안 쳐요.
소주를 못 마셔요./소주를 안 마셔요.
사진을 못 찍어요./사진을 안 찍어요.
운전 못 해요./운전 안 해요.
태권도를 못 해요./태권도를 안 해요.

Page 228–229
가 수영을 할 수 있어요?
나 네, 저는 수영을 할 수 있어요.
가 삼계탕을 먹을 수 있어요?
나 네, 저는 삼계탕을 먹을 수 있어요.
가 김치를 담글 수 있어요?
나 네, 저는 김치를 담글 수 있어요.
가 스키를 탈 수 있어요?
나 네, 저는 스키를 탈 수 있어요.
가 운전을 할 수 있어요?
나 네, 저는 운전을 할 수 있어요.

Pages 230–231
가 운전을 할 수 있어요?
나 저는 운전을 못 해요.
가 소주를 마실 수 있어요?
나 아니요, 저는 소주를 못 마셔요.
가 피아노를 칠 수 있어요?
나 아니요, 저는 피아노를 못 쳐요.
가 바이킹을 탈 수 있어요?
나 아니요, 저는 바이킹을 못 타요.
가 불고기를 만들 수 있어요?
나 아니요, 저는 불고기를 못 만들어요.

Vocabulary Index

가게 **gage** *store*

가깝다 **gakkapda** *to be close*

가루약 **garuyak** *powdered medicine*

가루약을 먹다 **garuyageul meokda** *to take medicine in powdered form*

가방을 들다 **gabangeul deulda** *to carry a bag*

가방을 메다 **gabangeul meda** *to carry a backpack*

가볍다 **gabyeopda** *to be light*

가수 **gasu** *singer*

가슴 **gaseum** *chest, breast*

가야금을 배우다 **gayageumeul baeuda** *to learn how to play the gayageum*

가을 **gaeul** *fall, autumn*

간병인 **ganbyeongin** *caregiver*

간호사 **ganhosa** *nurse*

감 **gam** *persimmon*

감기 **gamgi** *cold*

감기에 걸리다 **gamgie geollida** *to catch a cold*

감자탕 **gamjatang** *gamjatang (pork bone and potato stew)*

같이 **gachi** *together, with someone*

거리 **geori** *street, distance*

걱정하다 **geokjeonghada** *to worry*

건강에 좋다 **geongange jota** *to be good for one, to be healthy*

건너다 **geonneoda** *to cross*

걷다 **geotda** *to walk*

걸리다 **geollida** *to take (a certain amount of time)*

검도 **geomdo** *kendo*

검도를 하다 **geomdoreul hada** *to practice kendo*

겨울 **gyeoul** *winter*

결혼하다 **gyeolhonhada** *to marry*

경주 **gyeongju** *Gyeongju (city)*

경찰관 **gyeongchalgwan** *police officer*

계세요 **gyeseyo** *She/he is here*

계시다 **gyesida** *to be (somewhere, honorific)*

계절 **gyejeol** *seasons*

계획 **gyehoek** *a plan*

고등학생 **godeunghaksaeng** *high school student*

고모 **gomo** *aunt (father's sister)*

고소하다 **gosohada** *to be savory, to be nutty*

고향 **gohyang** *hometown*

곧장 **gotjang** *straight ahead, right away*

골목 **golmok** *alley*

골프를 치다 **golpeureul chida** *to play golf*

공무원 **gongmuwon** *government employee*

공중전화 **gongjungjeonhwa** *public payphone*

공짜 **gongjja** *free, to cost nothing*

공터 **gongteo** *vacant lot*

과일 **gwail** *fruit*

광장 **gwangjang** *square, plaza*

광주 **gwangju** *Gwangju (city)*

괜찮다 **gwaenchanta** *to be OK, to be alright*

괴롭다 **goeropda** *to be in pain, to be distressed*

교보문고 **gyobomungo** *Kyobo Bookstore*

교보빌딩 **gyobobilding** *Kyobo Building*

교수 **gyosu** *professor*

교통 **gyotong** *traffic*

귀 **gwi** *ear*

귀걸이 **gwigeori** *earrings*

귀엽다 **gwiyeopda** *to be cute*

귤 **gyul** *tangerine*

그냥 **geunyang** *just, as something is*

그대로 **geudaero** *as it is, without any change*

그래서 **geuraeseo** *so, for that reason*

그리고 **geurigo** *and, also*

그림을 그리다 **geurimeul geurida** *to draw a picture*

근처 **geuncheo** *the area, the vicinity*

글쎄요 **geulsseyo** *I'm not sure (used to avoid answering a question)*

기다리다 **gidarida** *to wait*

기분이 나쁘다 **gibuni nappeuda** *to feel bad, to be in a bad mood*

기분이 좋다 **gibuni jota** *to feel good, to be in a good mood*

기숙사 **gisuksa** *dormitory*

기차 **gicha** *train*

기침이 나다 **gichimi nada** *to have a cough*

길 **gil** *road, way*

길거리 **gilgeori** *street, road*

길다 **gilda** *to be long*

김밥집 **gimbapjip** *gimbap diner*

김치 **gimchi** *kimchi*

김치를 담그다 **gimchireul damgeuda** *to make kimchi*

까맣다 **kkamata** *black*

깜짝 놀라다 **kkamjjak nollada** *to be surprised*

깨다 **kkaeda** *to break, to wake up*

꽃무늬 **kkonmunui** *flower-print design*

끝나다 **kkeunnada** *to come to an end*

ㄴ

나쁘다 **nappeuda** *to be bad*

난타 **nanta** *Nanta (a percussion show)*

날씨 **nalssi** *weather*

날씬하다 **nalssinhada** *to be skinny*

남동생 **namdongsaeng** *younger brother*

남매 **nammae** *brother and sister*

남원 **namwon** *Namwon (city)*

남이섬 **namiseom** *Nami Island (tourist destination outside of Seoul)*

남자답다 **namjadapda** *to be manly, to be masculine*

남자 친구 **namja chingu** *boyfriend*

내과 **naegwa** *internal medicine*

냉면 **naengmyeon** *naengmyeon (cold noodles)*

넘어지다 **neomeojida** *to fall down*

네 번째 **ne beonjjae** *fourth*

넥타이 **nektai** *necktie*

넥타이를 매다 **nektaireul maeda** *to wear a necktie*

노랗다 **norata** *yellow*

노래방 **noraebang** *karaoke*

놀라다 **nollada** *to be surprised*

놀이터 **noriteo** *playground*

농구를 하다 **nonggureul hada** *to play basketball*

높다 **nopda** *to be high*

누구세요 **nuguseyo** *Who is this?*

누나 **nuna** *older sister (of a male)*

눈 **nun** *eye*

눈물이 나다 **nunmuri nada** *to have watery eyes*

눈병 **nunbyeong** *eye trouble*

눈사람 **nunsaram** *snowman*

눈싸움 **nunssaum** *snowball fight*

눈썰매 **nunsseolmae** *sled*

눈썰매를 타다 **nunsseolmaereul tada** *to ride a sled*

눈썰매장 **nunsseolmaejang** *a slope for sledding*

눈이 아프다 **nuni apeuda** *one's eyes hurt*

눕다 **nupda** *to lie down*

늦잠을 자다 **neutjameul jada** *to sleep in*

ㄷ

다니다 **danida** *to go somewhere regularly, to attend*

다리 **dari** *leg*

다리가 아프다 **dariga apeuda** *to have a sore leg*

다섯 번째 **daseot beonjjae** *fifth*

다시 전화하겠습니다 **dasi jeonhwahagetseumnida** *I will call again*

다이어트에 좋다 **daieoteue jota** *to help with one's diet*

단풍 **danpung** *autumn leaves (when the colors change)*

닫다 **datda** *to shut*

달다 **dalda** *to be sweet*

달콤하다 **dalkomhada** *to be sweet*

닭갈비 **dakgalbi** *dalkgalbi (pan-fried chicken)*

담배를 피우다 **dambaereul piuda** *to smoke a cigarette*

담백하다 **dambaekada** *to be mild*

대각선 **daegakseon** *diagonal line*

대기업 **daegieop** *large company, conglomerate*

대전 **daejeon** *Daejeon (city)*

대학생 **daehaksaeng** *university student*

대한항공 **daehanhanggong** *Korean Air*

대형마트 **daehyeongmateu** *supermarket*

댁 **daek** *house (honorific)*

덥다 **deopda** *to be hot*

도시 **dosi** *city*

도시락을 먹다 **dosirageul meokda** *to eat a packed lunch*

도와주다 **dowajuda** *to help*

도착하다 **dochakada** *to arrive, to get (somewhere)*

돈가스 **dongaseu** *pork cutlet*

돈이 많다 **doni manta** *to have a lot of money*

돌다 **dolda** *to turn*

돌아오다 **doraoda** *to come back, to return*

동대문 시장 **dongdaemun sijang** *Dongdaemun Market*

돼지고기 **dwaejigogi** *pork*

된장찌개 **doenjangjjigae** *doenjang jjigae (fermented soybean stew)*

두 번째 **du beonjjae** *second (number)*

뒤 **dwi** *behind*

드럼을 치다 **deureomeul chida** *to play a drum*

드림 **deurim** *"from" in a letter*

등 **deung** *back*

등산을 하다 **deungsaneul hada** *to go hiking*

디자이너 **dijaineo** *designer*

딸 **ttal** *daughter*

떡 **tteok** *rice cake*

떡볶이 **tteokbokki** *tteokbokki*

떫다 **tteolda** *to be bitter*

똑똑하다 **ttokttokada** *to be smart*

똑바로 **ttokbaro** *straight ahead, correctly*

뚱뚱하다 **ttungttunghada** *to be fat*

뛰다 **ttwida** *to run, to jump*

레깅스 **regingseu** *leggings*

레스토랑 **reseutorang** *restaurant (classy)*

록 페스티벌 **rok peseutibeol** *rock festival*

링거 **ringgeo** *IV drip*

마을 **maeul** *village, town*

마인츠 대학교 **maincheu daehakgyo** *Mainz University*

막히다 **makida** *to be blocked (often used to talk about traffic jams)*

만나다 **mannada** *to meet*

만지다 **manjida** *to touch*

만화를 읽다 **manhwareul ikda** *to read a comic book*

많다 **manta** *to be many, to be a lot of*

많이 **mani** *a lot*

말이 많다 **mari manta** *to be talkative*

말이 없다 **mari eopda** *to not say much*

맛 **mat** *flavors*

맞은편 **majeunpyeon** *the opposite side*

매력 없다 **maeryeok eopda** *to be unattractive*

매력 있다 **maeryeok itda** *to be attractive*

매출이 늘다 **maechuri neulda** *business sales increase*

매출이 줄다 **maechuri julda** *business sales decrease*

매콤하다 **maekomhada** *to be a little hot*

맵다 **maepda** *to be spicy*

맹장 **maengjang** *appendix*

머리 **meori** *head*

머리가 나쁘다 **meoriga nappeuda** *to be stupid*

머리가 아프다 **meoriga apeuda** *to have a headache*

머리가 좋다 **meoriga jota** *to be smart*

머리띠 **meoritti** *headband*

머리핀 **meoripin** *hairpin*

먹기가 편하다 **meokgiga pyeonhada**
  to be easy to eat

멀다 **meolda** *to be far*

멋있다 **meositda** *to look good, to be stylish*

멜론 **mellon** *melon*

메스껍다 **meseukkeopda** *to feel nauseous*

명 **myeong** *person (counting word)*

몇 명 **myeot myeong** *how many people*

모두 **modu** *altogether, all*

모자 **moja** *hat*

모자를 쓰다 **mojareul sseuda** *to wear a hat*

목 **mok** *throat*

목감기 **mokgamgi** *sore throat (caused by a cold)*

목걸이 **mokgeori** *necklace*

목구멍 **mokgumeong** *throat (inside)*

몸살감기 **momsalgamgi** *aching all over
  (caused by a cold)*

못 **mot** *cannot*

못되다 **motdoeda** *to be mean, to be bad*

못생기다 **motsaenggida** *to be ugly*

무뚝뚝하다 **muttukttukada** *to be curt, to be brusque*

무릎 **mureup** *knee*

무섭다 **museopda** *to be afraid*

물방울무늬 **mulbangulmunui** *polka-dot pattern*

물약 **mullyak** *liquid medicine*

물약을 먹다 **mullyageul meokda**
  to take medicine in liquid form

물파스 **mulpaseu** *liquid that helps with pain*

물파스를 바르다 **mulpaseureul bareuda**
  to apply liquid for pain relief

뮤지컬을 보다 **myujikeoreul boda** *to see a musical*

미안하다 **mianhada** *to be sorry*

바쁘다 **bappeuda** *to be busy*

바이킹을 타다 **baikingeul tada** *to ride the Viking
  (amusement park ride)*

바지 **baji** *pants*

박물관에 가다 **bangmulgwane gada**
  to go to a museum

반지 **banji** *ring*

반지를 끼다 **banjireul kkida** *to wear a ring*

반창고 **banchanggo** *band-aid*

반창고를 붙이다 **banchanggoreul buchida**
  to put on a band-aid

발 **bal** *foot*

발가락 **balgarak** *toe*

발꿈치 **balkkumchi** *heel*

발등 **baldeung** *instep*

발목 **balmok** *ankle*

발바닥 **balbadak** *sole of the foot*

발찌 **baljji** *anklet*

발톱 **baltop** *toenail*

밝다 **bakda** *to be bright, to be cheerful*

방송국 **bangsongguk** *broadcasting company*

방학 **banghak** *school vacation*

방학을 하다 **banghageul hada**
  to be on vacation from school

배 **bae** *stomach*

배가 아프다 **baega apeuda** *to have a stomachache*

배를 타다 **baereul tada** *to get on a boat*

배우다 **baeuda** *to learn*

백 번째 **baek beonjjae** *hundredth*

백화점 **baekwajeom** *department store*

버스 **beoseu** *bus*

버스정류장 **beoseujeongnyujang** *bus stop*

벌써 **beolsseo** *already*

벼룩시장 **byeoruksijang** *flea market*

알러지가 있다 **alleojiga itda** *to have an allergy*

알약 **allyak** *pill*

알약을 먹다 **allyageul meokda** *to take a pill*

앞 **ap** *in front of*

야구장에 가다 **yagujange gada** *to go to a baseball game*

야채가 많다 **yachaega manta** *there are a lot of vegetables*

약국 **yakguk** *pharmacy*

약사 **yaksa** *pharmacist*

약속이 있다 **yaksogi itda** *to already have plans*

약의 종류 **yagui jongnyu** *kinds of medicine*

양말 **yangmal** *socks*

양말을 신다 **yangmareul sinda** *to wear socks*

양복 **yangbok** *suit (for men)*

어깨 **eokkae** *shoulder*

어깨를 주무르다 **eokkaereul jumureuda** *to massage someone's shoulders*

어떤 사람 **eotteon saram** *what kind of person*

어리다 **eorida** *to be young*

어머니 **eomeoni** *mother*

어서 오세요 **eoseo oseyo** *please come in*

어울리다 **eoullida** *to look good (on someone)*

어지럽다 **eojireopda** *to feel dizzy*

여가 **yeoga** *leisure activities*

언니 **eonni** *older sister (of a female)*

얼굴 **eolgul** *face*

얼굴이 둥글다 **eolguri dunggeulda** *to have a round face*

엉덩이 **eongdeongi** *buttocks*

엔터테인먼트 **enteoteinmeonteu** *talent agencies*

여덟 번째 **yeodeol beonjjae** *eighth*

여동생 **yeodongsaeng** *younger sister*

여름 **yeoreum** *summer*

여보세요 **yeoboseyo** *Hello? (when answering the phone)*

여섯 번째 **yeoseot beonjjae** *sixth*

여자 친구 **yeoja chingu** *girlfriend*

연고 **yeongo** *ointment*

연고를 바르다 **yeongoreul bareuda** *to apply ointment*

연극을 보다 **yeongeugeul boda** *to see a play*

연예인 **yeonyein** *celebrity*

열 번째 **yeol beonjjae** *tenth*

열다 **yeolda** *to open*

열이 나다 **yeori nada** *to have a fever*

영화감독 **yeonghwagamdok** *movie director*

영화사 **yeonghwasa** *film studio*

예쁘다 **yeppeuda** *to be pretty*

오랜만이에요 **oraenmanieyo** *It has been a long time*

오른쪽 **oreunjjok** *the right side*

오빠 **oppa** *older brother (of a female)*

오한이 나다 **ohani nada** *to have chills*

올해 **olhae** *this year*

옷 **ot** *clothing*

옷을 입다 **oseul ipda** *to wear (clothing)*

와이셔츠 **waisyeocheu** *dress shirt*

왕의 남자 **wangui namja** *The King and the Clown (Korean movie starring Lee Joon-gi)*

왜 **wae** *why*

외과 **oegwa** *surgery*

외교관 **oegyogwan** *diplomat*

외모 **oemo** *appearance*

외할머니 **oehalmeoni** *maternal grandmother*

외할아버지 **oeharabeoji** *maternal grandfather*

왼쪽 **oenjjok** *the left side*

요가 **yoga** *yoga*

요즘 **yojeum** *lately, these days*

우체부 **uchebu** *postman*

우회전하다 **uhoejeonhada** *to turn right*

운전하다 **unjeonhada** *to drive*

울다 **ulda** *to cry*

웃다 **utda** *to smile*

원피스 **wonpiseu** *dress*

원피스를 입다 **wonpiseureul ipda** *to wear a dress*

위장 **wijang** *stomach*

위치 **wichi** *direction*

유치원생 **yuchiwonsaeng** *kindergarten student*

유턴하다 **yuteonhada** *to make a U-turn*

육교 **yukgyo** *pedestrian bridge*

은행원 **eunhaengwon** *bank clerk*

음식 **eumsik** *food*

음악을 듣다 **eumageul deutda** *to listen to music (lit., to appreciate music)*

의료진 **uiryojin** *medical professionals*

의사 **uisa** *doctor*

이 **i** *tooth*

이가 아프다 **iga apeuda** *to have a toothache*

이럴 때 **ireol ttae** *at a time like this*

이메일 **imeil** *email*

이모 **imo** *aunt (mother's sister)*

이비인후과 **ibiinhugwa** *ENT (ear, nose and throat)*

이유 **iyu** *reasons*

인도 **indo** *sidewalk*

인사동 **insadong** *Insadong (Seoul neighborhood popular with tourists)*

인천 **incheon** *Incheon (city)*

일곱 번째 **ilgop beonjjae** *seventh*

일등을 하다 **ildeungeul hada** *to come in first place*

일이 끝나다 **iri kkeunnada** *work is over*

일하다 **ilhada** *to work*

입 **ip** *mouth*

있다 **itda** *to be (somewhere), to have*

ㅈ

자꾸 **jakku** *repeatedly, again and again*

자동차 **jadongcha** *automobile*

자매 **jamae** *sisters*

자전거를 타다 **jajeongeoreul tada** *to ride a bicycle*

작가 **jakga** *writer*

작곡가 **jakgokga** *songwriter*

작년 **jangnyeon** *last year*

작다 **jakda** *to be small*

작사가 **jaksaga** *lyricist*

잘 **jal** *well (as in "to do something well")*

잘생기다 **jalsaenggida** *to be handsome*

잠시만 기다리세요 **jamsiman gidariseyo** *just a moment*

잠을 자다 **jameul jada** *to sleep*

장갑 **janggap** *gloves*

장갑을 끼다 **janggabeul kkida** *to wear gloves*

장소 **jangso** *a place*

재미없다 **jaemieopda** *to not be fun, to be uninteresting*

재미있다 **jaemiitda** *to be fun, to be interesting*

재채기가 나다 **jaechaegiga nada** *to sneeze*

재킷 **jaket** *suit jacket, blazer*

전시실 **jeonsisil** *exhibition room*

전주 한옥마을 **jeonju hanongmaeul** *Jeonju Hanok Village*

정도 **jeongdo** *about, approximately*

정동진 **jeongdongjin** *Jeongdongjin*

정장 **jeongjang** *suit (for women)*

정장을 입다 **jeongjangeul ipda** *to wear formal attire*

제주도 **jejudo** *Jeju Island*

조금 **jogeum** *a little*

조용하다 **joyonghada** *to be quiet*

졸업하다 **joreopada** *to graduate (from school)*

좌회전하다 **jwahoejeonhada** *to turn left*

주사 **jusa** *a shot, injection*

주점 **jujeom** *bar (for drinking), pub*

주치의 **juchiui** *family physician*

준기 손잡고 **jungi sonjapgo** *Holding Hands with Joon-gi (yearly concert)*

준비하다 **junbihada** *to prepare, to get ready*

줄무늬 **julmunui** *stripe*

중앙선 **jungangseon** *center line (on the road)*

중학생 **junghaksaeng** *middle school student*

즐겁다 **jeulgeopda** *to be enjoyable, to be fun, to be pleasant*

증상 **jeungsang** *various symptoms*

지갑 **jigap** *wallet*

지내다 **jinaeda** *to spend time, to be (as in the expression "how have you been")*

지루하다 **jiruhada** *to be boring*

지하도 **jihado** *underground walkway*

지하철역 **jihacheollyeok** *subway station*

지휘자 **jihwija** *conductor (of an orchestra)*

직업 **jigeop** *job*

직진하다 **jikjinhada** *to go straight*

집 **jip** *house*

집이 멀다 **jibi meolda** *my house is far away*

짜다 **jjada** *to be salty*

짧다 **jjalda** *to be short*

쫄면 **jjolmyeon** *jjolmyeon (noodle dish)*

쭉 **jjuk** *straight ahead*

찜닭 **jjimdak** *jjimdalk (steamed chicken)*

착하다 **chakada** *to be nice*

참 **cham** *really, truly*

처방전 **cheobangjeon** *prescription*

천 번째 **cheon beonjjae** *thousandth*

첫 번째 **cheot beonjjae** *first*

청바지 **cheongbaji** *jeans*

청와대 **cheongwadae** *The Blue House (where the Korean president lives)*

체육관 **cheyukgwan** *gymnasium*

초대장 **chodaejang** *an invitation*

초대장을 보내다 **chodaejangeul bonaeda** *to send an invitation*

초등학생 **chodeunghaksaeng** *elementary school student*

초콜릿 **chokollit** *chocolate*

촬영하다 **chwaryeonghada** *to shoot (a movie)*

출발하다 **chulbalhada** *to set out, to depart*

춥다 **chupda** *to be cold*

취업 준비 **chwieop junbi** *to look for a job*

취직하다 **chwijikada** *to get a job, to be hired*

치과 **chigwa** *dentistry*

치마 **chima** *skirt*

친구를 돕다 **chingureul dopda** *to help one's friends*

친절하다 **chinjeolhada** *to be kind, to be friendly*

침대 **chimdae** *bed*

침대에 눕다 **chimdaee nupda** *to lie in bed*

카메라 **kamera** *camera*

카페 **kape** *café*

칼국수 **kalguksu** *kalguksu (noodle dish)*

코 **ko** *nose*

코가 막히다 **koga makida** *to have a stuffy nose*

코감기 **kogamgi** *runny nose (caused by a cold)*

코트 **koteu** *coat*

콘서트에 가다 **konseoteue gada** *to go to a concert*

콧물이 나다 **konmuri nada** *to have a runny nose*

키가 작다 **kiga jakda** *to be short*

키가 크다 **kiga keuda** *to be tall*

탈춤을 추다 **talchumeul chuda** *to perform a mask dance*

탕수육 **tangsuyuk** *sweet-and-sour pork*

태권도를 하다 **taegwondoreul hada** *to practice taekwondo*

테니스를 치다 **teniseureul chida** *to play tennis*

토하다 **tohada** *to throw up*

통역관 **tongyeokgwan** *interpreter*

투명인간 **tumyeongingan** *invisible man*

티셔츠 **tisyeocheu** *T-shirt*

파랗다 **parata** *blue*

파스 **paseu** *pain-relief patch*

파스를 붙이다 **paseureul buchida** *to put on a pain-relief patch*

파인애플 **painaepeul** *pineapple*

팔 **pal** *arm*

팔꿈치 **palkkumchi** *elbow*

팔찌 **paljji** *bracelet*

편의점 **pyeonuijeom** *convenience store*

평창 **pyeongchang** *Pyeongchang*

폐 **pye** *lungs*

포도 **podo** *grapes*

표지판 **pyojipan** *street sign*

푹 **puk** *a lot, well (often used with 쉬다)*

풍선 **pungseon** *balloon*

피가 나다 **piga nada** *to bleed*

피곤하다 **pigonhada** *to be tired*

피아노를 치다 **pianoreul chida** *to play the piano*

피아니스트 **pianiseuteu** *pianist*

핑계 **pinggye** *excuses*

하늘 **haneul** *sky*

하다 **hada** *to do*

하얗다 **hayata** *white*

하의 **haui** *bottoms, pants*

하의를 입다 **hauireul ipda** *to wear pants (lit., a bottom)*

하지만 **hajiman** *but, however*

한국 민속촌 **hanguk minsokchon** *Korean Folk Village*

한국의 회사 **hangugui hoesa** *major companies in Korea*

한 번도 **han beondo** *not once*

한라산 **hallasan** *Halla Mountain*

한마디만 **hanmadiman** *Only One Word (song by Lee Joon-gi)*

할머니 **halmeoni** *grandmother*

할아버지 **harabeoji** *grandfather*

항공사 **hanggongsa** *airline*

행복하다 **haengbokada** *to be happy*

허리 **heori** *waist, lower back*

허리띠 **heoritti** *belt*

헤어지다 **heeojida** *to break up, to separate*

헤이리 **heiri** *Heyri (name of a village)*

혀 **hyeo** *tongue*

형 **hyeong** *older brother (of a male)*

현대 **hyeondae** *Hyundai*

형제 **hyeongje** *brothers*

호떡을 팔다 **hotteogeul palda** *to sell hotteok (sweet, sticky pancakes)*

홍대 **hongdae** *Hongdae (university neighborhood in Seoul)*

화가 **hwaga** *painter*

환자 **hwanja** *patient*

회사원 **hoesawon** *office worker*

횡단보도 **hoengdanbodo** *crosswalk*

휴게실 **hyugesil** *rest area*

휴대폰 **hyudaepon** *mobile phone*

휴일 **hyuil** *a day off*

휴지를 줍다 **hyujireul jupda** *to pick up trash (lit., to pick up tissue)*

힘들다 **himdeulda** *to be hard*

Published by Tuttle Publishing, an imprint of Periplus Editions (HK) Ltd.

www.tuttlepublishing.com

이준기와 함께하는 안녕하세요 한국어 2
Copyright © Maribooks, 2013.
Originally published in Korea by Maribooks.
English translation rights arranged with
Maribooks in care of Danny Hong Agency, Seoul.

English translation copyright © 2024 Periplus Editions (HK) Ltd.

Library of Congress Control Number in progress

ISBN 978-0-8048-5621-8
Distributed by
North America, Latin America & Europe
Tuttle Publishing
364 Innovation Drive
North Clarendon,
VT 05759-9436 U.S.A.
Tel: 1 (802) 773-8930
Fax: 1 (802) 773-6993
info@tuttlepublishing.com
www.tuttlepublishing.com

Asia Pacific
Berkeley Books Pte. Ltd.
3 Kallang Sector #04-01
Singapore 349278
Tel: (65) 6741-2178
Fax: (65) 6741-2179
inquiries@periplus.com.sg
www.tuttlepublishing.com

27 26 25 24   5 4 3 2 1
Printed in China   2401EP

TUTTLE PUBLISHING® is a registered trademark of Tuttle Publishing, a division of
Periplus Editions (HK) Ltd.